Crushing

God Turns Pressure into Power

STUDY GUIDE

T. D. JAKES

FaithWords

New York Nashville

FaithWords
Hachette Book Group
1290 Avenue of the Americas, New York, NY 10104
faithwords.com
twitter.com/faithwords

First edition: April 2019

FaithWords is a division of Hachette Book Group, Inc. The FaithWords name and logo are trademarks of Hachette Book Group, Inc.

The publisher is not responsible for websites (or their content) that are not owned by the publisher.

The Hachette Speakers Bureau provides a wide range of authors for speaking events. To find out more, go to www.hachettespeakersbureau.com or call (866) 376-6591.

ISBN: 9781546010555 (trade paperback)

Printed in the United States of America

LSC-C

10 9 8 7 6 5 4 3 2 1

Contents

Contents

Introduction

Thank you for choosing to enhance your engagement with my book *Crushing: God Turns Pressure into Power* through your interaction with this study guide. Suffering is an inherently painful and deeply personal experience, and while I cannot alleviate the source of your life's heartaches, I pray that through this guide you would be comforted, consoled, and encouraged to consider the spiritual purposes of our individual crushings.

The material in this guide is designed to help you integrate and apply the wisdom of God's Word along with the humble gleaning of my own experiences. Ultimately, how you use this guide is up to you, but my hope is that it will complement your understanding and personalization of the lessons in crushing in ways both profound and practical. You may want to work through the study guide as you read each chapter of the book, use it as a catalyst for fruitful discussion in your small group or book club, or experience it as a devotional companion. The format here follows each chapter of the book with additional insight, questions for spiritual reflection, and exercises intended to shift the way you think about some of the most crushing moments in your life.

I've crafted this guide to pair with the book in ways that will address a variety of life's hardest moments. Knowing this in advance, you may want to read through this guide and the book prior to discussing the material with others in order to allow yourself time to process, reflect, and integrate my message. A private reading also enables you to take as much time as you want or need in order to spend time in prayer and seek God's healing, guidance, and restoration. In order to get the most out of this experience, I strongly encourage you to regard the questions seriously and to be as honest and specific as possible in your responses. Remember, no one needs to see anything you choose to write in these pages except you and God.

After taking adequate time to absorb and reflect on the radical and sometimes shocking perspectives I propose on the purposes of crushing in our lives, you will discover that sharing your thoughts and feelings within a group setting can amplify the material's impact. Knowing others' responses are uniquely personal and deeply held, please respect the pain, power, and process of crushing that they choose to reveal with you and other group members. Seek to facilitate healing, growth, and renewal as you empower one another. Avoid criticism and judgment, and always uphold the boundaries of privacy to which your group has agreed to adhere.

My prayer is that this guide will bless you in unexpected ways so that you might shift your views on the times you have endured crushing events. As you will see, new wine emerges when we learn the powerful truth that God turns pressure into power.

CHAPTER 1

When Everything Falls Apart

If you are reading my book *Crushing* and have now decided to supplement your engagement with its message by completing this study guide, then you have likely already considered the nature of suffering in your life. After all, crushing blows happen to all of us, no matter the color of our skin, level of our education, or the amount in our bank account. No one is exempt from pain in this life, nor should we expect to be inoculated against the ongoing consequences that crushing causes in our soul. Everyone I know who matures in their faith and perseveres successfully in their life comes to terms with being crushed—and moving forward again.

I begin this book with one of the most challenging seasons of my life: having my young daughter Sarah reveal she was soon to be a mother shortly after I grieved the passing of my own mother. My entire world seemed upside down. On either side of me generationally, I mourned the loss of two pillars in my life—the loving presence of my mother and the precious innocence of my daughter.

I felt as if the ground had opened up beneath me and my steps were suddenly mired in quicksand. Everything around me seemed to move in slow motion, even as my mind raced with myriad thoughts and my heart pounded from the prompting of adrenaline coursing through my exhausted body. There was never a question of abandoning my faith in God; it was simply a matter of trying to reorient myself to this new configuration of life circumstances. I felt crushed but desperately prayed that it was not the end—of me, of my family, of my ministry.

1) When have you received news that left you reeling? How did you handle receiving it in the moment? How would you handle similar, life-changing news differently today? Why?

_____

_____

_____

_____

2) Which of the following emotions have you felt when everything has appeared to fall apart in your life? Check all that apply. After you've considered all of these, circle the three that felt most powerful during this trial.

_____ Shock

_____ Fear

_____ Anger

_____ Confusion

_____ Disappointment

_____ Shame

_____ Sadness

_____ Despair

_____ Anxiety

_____ Detachment

_____ Denial

_____ Regret

_____ Paralysis/uncertainty

_____ Something else: _____

When your life suddenly falls apart, you may feel like you're freefalling into space, suddenly untethered by the constants you used to know in life that are suddenly no longer in place. Your health, your life, your relationships, your finances, your career are all revealed to be much more fragile than you ever realized. No longer do you have the security, peace, and stability you once took for granted.

When everything falls apart suddenly in your life, you may also feel confused by the way something so devastating can occur in the midst of a season that has otherwise been productive and successful. It may even be tempting to allow the painful pivot points to outweigh your achievements along with your ascension in other areas of your life. But life doesn't stop even though you feel like it has. Instead, you have to decide how you will handle the bittersweet blend of terror and triumph.

1) How have you managed to maintain perspective during past moments of crisis in your life? Do you tend to remain calm as you slowly absorb the new reality and decide how to respond? Or have you usually reacted in a more explosive expression of your immediate emotions?

_____

_____

_____

_____

2) Is it easier for you to see the big picture and maintain a long-term perspective on your life or to see what needs to be done only in the immediate, short-term present moment? How do your default tendencies help you process life's challenges?

_____

_____

_____

_____

_____

When your life seems to fall apart, you inevitably, like most of us, begin to seek an understanding of your situation—its cause, its concentration, and its consequences. Often during this attempt to process pain, we discover the strength and durability of our personal faith. It's easy to trust God when your family is healthy, your career is flourishing, and your bills are paid. But when everything falls apart, the confidence you once had in God's goodness is suddenly as fragile as your broken heart.

Questions suddenly replace certainty, and doubt becomes an insistent moth eating away at the fabric of your faith. We wonder how our lives can be such a strange mixture of blessing and bereavement, of discovery and disintegration, of gain and grief. No one has all the answers, but I remain convinced that asking our questions and investigating our life's trajectory is an essential part of personal and spiritual growth. As we see in Jesus' parable below, we must be willing to endure the weeds as we grow our seeds:

> The kingdom of heaven is like a man who sowed good seed in his field. But while everyone was sleeping, his enemy came and sowed weeds among the wheat, and went away. When the wheat sprouted and formed heads, then the weeds also appeared.
>
> The owner's servants came to him and said, "Sir, didn't you sow good seed in your field? Where then did the weeds come from?"
>
> "An enemy did this," he replied.
>
> The servants asked him, "Do you want us to go and pull them up?"
>
> "No," he answered, "because while you are pulling the weeds, you may uproot the wheat with them. Let both grow together until the harvest. At that time I will tell the harvesters: First collect the weeds and tie them in bundles to be burned; then gather the wheat and bring it into my barn."
>
> (Matt. 13:24–30)

Pursuing our divine destiny, we plant seeds of faith to produce a fruitful harvest only to discover weeds of doubt, disappointment, and despair threatening our productivity. We know, however, that God is all powerful, all knowing, and all loving so we struggle to reconcile our grasp of His character with the harsh reality of weeds in our life's garden.

Consequently, we must dare to consider that God is so powerful, so good, and so loving that He can somehow take life's weeds and use them to make us stronger, wiser, and more dependent on Him.

1) What events in your life have caused you to wrestle with doubts about your relationship with God and your understanding of His character? How have you handled such concerns in the past? Have you usually expressed your questions and pulled away from God? Or have you tended to keep them to yourself as you attempt to grind your way forward?

_____

_____

_____

_____

2) How has Jesus' parable of the "weeds and seeds" (Matt. 13:24–30) played out in your own life? When have you experienced trouble in the midst of doing what you know God has called you to do? Have you tried to pull those weeds right away, or have you chosen to wait and deal with them later?

_____

_____

_____

_____

3) How do you believe God views the coexistence of His peace in the midst of our pain? How have you typically answered the question of why we suffer so much loss even as we

serve a loving, generous God? Why would a good Father allow His children to suffer so much pain, injustice, and heartache?

_____

_____

_____

_____

In the midst of our grappling, we want to believe the promise expressed in the Bible: "And we know that in all things God works for the good of those who love him, who have been called according to his purpose" (Rom. 8:28). The tricky part here, of course, is that this verse says _all_ things—not just the good things or the things we choose, but all things. Keeping all things in mind then, we must include our darkest, most desperate moments, those times that seem so brutal, unbearable, and crushing.

All things must include the personal losses that you're grieving at this very moment, the pain you carry around inside you daily. _All_ includes your life's disappointment, devastation, and destruction, and the events, situations, and conversations that forever change the shape of your soul. How is it that God works for your good even in the midst of those times of crushing?

That question is the centerpiece of my book. Even as God has equipped, educated, and empowered you to stride boldly into your future, you must also endure the crushing moments that seem to undermine everything you work so hard to produce. Is it possible that God is somehow using the interplay of those two forces as a catalyst of growth and greater productivity in your life?

If you're willing to open your mind and your heart to such a radical possibility, you may discover that you have been limited in your comprehension of God's purpose for your life. While you may be focused on smaller, short-term gains, your Creator is intent on growing you for His eternal purposes. Shifting your paradigm, however, requires you to change the way you have always viewed the worst moments of your life.

1) Being completely honest, do you *really* believe "that in all things God works for the good of those who love him" (Rom. 8:28)? What are some of your life's "all things" that you struggle to reconcile with God's purpose and plan for your life?

_____

_____

_____

_____

2) What events in your life will you always struggle to understand or see as part of God's ultimate plan for your life? How can you surrender even these losses, wounds, and grievances to God as you seek to grow stronger in your faith? Can you see how surrendering them is essential to your ability to gain a new perspective on why God allows such times of crushing in your life?

_____

_____

_____

_____

3) What feelings are stirred within you as you consider revising the way you see your life's hardest times and greatest losses? Do you feel more resistant or more relieved? More skeptical or more hopeful? Why?

_____

_____

_____

_____

Crushing places in our life ultimately reveal there's more to our lives than what we can see. There's more in the midst of those times than we can plan, expect, control, or understand on our own. Times of soul-crushing doubt and suffering compel us to seek God for a sense of comfort, comprehension, and counsel.

When we seek His guidance and follow His voice, then our crushing becomes the creation of something new. To find a metaphor, we only have to look at how tons of rock and soil crush carbon deposits within the earth into diamonds. From the carbon's perspective, it must seem like the weight of the world will destroy its essence. But in the process, we can see that such crushing weight results in something new and precious, something that could never be attained without that intense weight bearing down on the carbon.

An even more potent comparison for our process comes from the Bible. In both the Old and New Testaments, we see references to the process of winemaking that I find curiously similar to the nuanced stages of our personal growth and development. In Scripture, we discover so many descriptions, images, metaphors, and parables related to the agrarian culture of ancient times. Consequently, we can see the way planting, tending, gardening, harvesting, and fermenting traces the journey of grape to wine in ways that parallel our own growth, productivity, crushing, and release.

1) In theory, can you see the way crushing might be the way God takes us to the next level in our growth in development? Based on those times when everything has fallen apart in your own life, however, what hinders your acceptance of this premise emotionally, intellectually, and spiritually?

_____

_____

_____

_____

2) When you think about the way planting, growing, farming, and harvesting is mentioned so frequently in the Bible, what images, verses, or passages come to mind? How have they given you strength in times past? How do they fit within this notion of crushing as part of God's process for unleashing who you were meant to be?

_____

_____

_____

_____

The hardest part of shifting the way we view suffering in our lives often revolves around how we view our life's purpose. We tend to view our fruit as what we can see, enjoy, accomplish, attain, and conquer. But God considers our fruit to be spiritual and eternal in nature, which results in the transformation of our earthly fruit into His eternal wine. Our suffering is not the end of our accomplishments—in many ways, it is only the beginning.

Making wine, however, takes time. The seeds have to be planted and watered, weeded and tended. The fruit has to grow and be picked at peak ripeness. The grapes must be sorted so that those that are spoiled or sour are eliminated before the fruit is crushed into juice. Then the process of fermentation requires time for the juice to become full with the flavors found in wine. Even once the wine has formed and been bottled, the beverage may not reach peak power and potency for many years.

You must view your process of transformation the same way. It takes time to deal with the blows of life that leave you reeling on the ground, wondering if you will ever walk again. It takes time to get back on your feet and begin moving forward again. It takes time to trust God at a deeper level and realize that He can indeed be trusted with every area of your life. It takes time to accept that *crushing is not the end*!

1) On a scale of 1 to 10, with 1 being completely unwilling and 10 being totally willing, how would you rate your openness to accepting that your crushing is part of God's maturation process for your life? What memories, scars, wounds, and worries shape the score you chose?

_____

_____

_____

_____

2) What obstacles, issues, and baggage from your past might hinder your ability to change the way you view crushing in your life? How can you release them in order to see clearly and open your heart more fully?

_____

_____

_____

_____

3) Are you willing to consider that your life's biggest failures, greatest losses, and darkest moments can be used by God for your good and for His glory? Why or why not?

_____

_____

_____

_____

CHAPTER 2

Quality Control

As I came to terms with the long-term consequences of losing my mother as well as gaining the new life my daughter Sarah was carrying, I often felt totally disoriented. While I continued to function on a daily basis, most nights found me staring out the windows in my home as tears coursed down my cheeks. I am a proactive, take-charge kind of person, and as this double punch of life circumstances left me feeling powerless, I didn't know how to move forward.

I knew I did not want to abandon my God-given calling to nurture faith in the lives of others, but I could not come to terms with why the Lord had allowed such soul-crushing events to occur in my life, and so close to one another. My spiritual navigation system no longer operated like I was accustomed to having. I went from being a modern traveler with a GPS to becoming a pioneer forced to return to basics of navigation. I needed to find new direction for my life as I struggled to discover the new path God had for me.

1) When was the last time you got lost while trying to reach an unfamiliar destination? What caused the challenge in your navigation? Were you relying on technology, directions provided by someone else, or your own sense of direction? How did you feel at the time as you attempted to reorient yourself and get back on track?

_____

_____

_____

_____

_____

2) How do the feelings of being lost on a physical journey parallel your feelings when life circumstances brought you to unfamiliar places? How do you typically respond when you find yourself feeling lost spiritually?

_____

_____

_____

_____

_____

As we explore in chapter 2 of *Crushing*, it takes time to produce quality results. Whether you're cooking a delicious meal, painting a portrait, or writing a novel, acts of creation necessitate giving oneself to the process rather than forcing the result to conform to our own timetable. So why should we expect anything else when our Creator shapes us as His masterpiece?

We are created in God's image, and He is the designer of everything inside us. Therefore, it seems logical for us to see His creativity expressed in our own designs and creations. God has planted gifts, talents, and abilities in us and wants to help cultivate them to full fruition and utilization. But this process of maturation takes time. It operates according to God's timing and not our own. Consequently, we often end up feeling impatient, frustrated, and confused when we can't align crushing circumstances in our lives with what we know to be our calling. Instead, God asks us to trust Him—and wait.

1) What do you produce or create in your own life that requires patience and care in order to produce quality? What happens when you attempt to rush the process? Why is embracing the process such an important part of your result?

_____

_____

_____

_____

_____

2) When have you experienced seasons or situations when sudden challenges seemed to interfere with the creation of something God had called you to do? It might have been launching a new ministry, starting a small business, initiating a new relationship, or making changes in your spending habits. How did you continue to complete your new endeavor despite those challenges?

_____

_____

_____

_____

Our relationship with God through Jesus is nowhere better expressed than in the metaphor Christ Himself gave to His disciples. While they had gathered together to celebrate the Passover meal, Jesus explained:

> I am the true vine, and my Father is the gardener. He cuts off every branch in me that bears no fruit, while every branch that does bear fruit he prunes so that it will be even more fruitful. You are already clean because of the word I have spoken to you. Remain in me, as I also remain in you. No branch can bear fruit by itself; it must remain in the vine. Neither can you bear fruit unless you remain in me.
>
> (John 15:1–4)

Jesus' metaphor here speaks directly to God's character, the reason Jesus came to earth in human form, our identity as God's children, and our Creator's master plan for reuniting us in relationship with Him. In this passage, I like the way some other translations use the word *vinedresser* instead of *gardener*. A vinedresser specifically cultivates grapevines and is responsible for the grapes' development and maturation into ripe fruit suitable for making wine. Based on Jesus' explanation here, we can see how God desires us to be branches connected to Him, the True Vine, in order to have life and nourishment that bears spiritual fruit.

This metaphor also reminds us that we're not capable of producing fruit by ourselves. We must be connected, nourished, and strengthened by Christ, our life-giving Vine, even as we serve the purposes of God, the Master Vinedresser. We each have potential inside us that can only bear fruit when we are connected spiritually to the source of our life and power.

1) Do you consider yourself to have a green thumb, as we say of someone who seems to have a knack for growing, cultivating, and tending to plants, flowers, and gardens? Or do you see yourself more as someone who struggles to keep a cactus alive? How does your ability to relate to gardening affect the way you understand this passage (John 15:1–4)?

_____

_____

_____

_____

2) Based on Jesus' description here, how would you explain God's role in the process of your spiritual growth and maturation? And how would you distinguish what God does in this process from the role that Jesus says he plays? Finally, what is our role in this process of cultivation?

_____

_____

The natural, physical phenomenon of birth, life, maturation, death, and rebirth reflects the pattern of spiritual development in our lives as well. Consequently, God sent Jesus to live on earth in human form to provide us with a perfect example of how to mature into the fullness of all that we were created to be.

Christ understood firsthand each of our trials, difficulties, and temptations. He experienced all the growth pains every human being experiences. He also demonstrated the process of moving from our present, temporary state of fruit bearing into the timeless, eternal harvest planted inside us. Just as a seed planted must die in order to move on to its next stage of development, we must also realize that we can never grow to complete fruition with a similar kind of surrender.

1) What do you consider to be the fruit of your life so far? What evidence would you provide to substantiate this fruit? What other fruit are you currently pursuing in your life? What stage or season of development is it in right now?

2) When you consider the events, good and bad, that have shaped your life the most, what three or four seem most influential? How did you view them at the time they happened? How has your perspective on them changed now as you look back? In other words, from your experience, how does the passing of time affect the way you see God at work in your life?

_____

_____

_____

_____

Just as we are called to be like Christ and to become like Him as we are called by God (1 Cor. 11:1), we must also embrace the necessity of our own similar growth process. Through this process of maturation, we realize there's more going on in our lives than we may have recognized at first. Our temporary fruit was never the endgame of our Vinedresser, but just another single step in the process of making us into His eternal wine. Our spiritual development from seeds to mature fruit-bearing branches requires us to grow out of life's dirty places.

Most of us don't like being in such muddy soil and often struggle to grab hold of something we hope will pull us out of our misery. We may try to regain our footing and recover a sense of balance by looking to other people, old habits, or addictive escapes. We know we're in trouble and don't like the vulnerable, fragile feelings that go with the cold, dark dirty places of life. We might justify giving in to temptations we know ultimately will not rescue us. We struggle and strive only to fall facedown in the mud again, left to face our own lonely discomfort.

1) When have you been in a dirty place in life most recently? What brought you to that point? How did you handle your distress at being brought so low?

_____

_____

_____

_____

2) When you have a bad day, one when everything that could go wrong seems to be worse than you imagined, how do you handle your pain, distress, anger, and frustration? What or whom do you reach for? How does this soothe or comfort you?

_____

_____

_____

_____

3) When a major crisis occurs, do you handle it much the same as you might handle a bad day? Or do you seek out other forms of relief, comfort, safety, or protection? How do you respond when your attempt to pull yourself out of your pit of misery fails?

_____

_____

_____

_____

Despite our discomfort, distress, and disappointment, God will not abandon His cultivation of us. He knows that if a seed is not planted, it will not grow. Seeds must be covered by the dirt and dung of life in order to grow roots and sprout new life above the surface. If we want to grow into the fullness of who God created us to be, then we must accept that dirty places are inevitable in our development.

No matter how harsh, stark, or dark our dirty places, we must realize that God is at work there. No place is ever too dirty for Him to use as the rich soil of your maturation and spiritual fruition. Perhaps it's time to reconsider the struggles, flaws, mistakes, and imperfections in your life and see them as positive parts of the process rather than negative interference in your growth. We have to remember that God is committed to the quality of our development, not our comfort and convenience.

1) When have you experienced the most spiritual growth in your life? What was the context or circumstances in which this growth took place? How did God use the manure of your mistakes to fertilize your own fecundity? What fruit do you continue to bear in your life from this period of prior growth?

_____

_____

_____

_____

2) What emotions do you associate with the dirty places of your life? Shame? Fear? Regret? Anger? Frustration? Something else?

_____

_____

_____

_____

3) Where have you found life-giving, spiritual nourishment during times in life's dirty places? How did these help you in the midst of your struggle? Check all that apply below.

_____ Reading the Bible
_____ Praying alone
_____ Praying with others
_____ Worshiping at church

_____ Meditating on Scripture
_____ Singing and listening to music
_____ Reading books or devotional material from favorite authors
_____ Confiding in a trusted confidant
_____ Spending time with family
_____ Other: _____

CHAPTER 3

The Strategy of Cultivation

In ancient mythology, a man named Sisyphus was punished for his crimes by forever rolling a rock up and down a mountain. Albert Camus, a twentieth-century existential philosopher and author, used Sisyphus as a symbol of human suffering and our feelings of futility when faced with our failures. A much more powerful story of enduring suffering speaks to me in the life of Nelson Mandela, the iconic South African leader. Mandela spent twenty-seven years imprisoned for taking a stand against the racial and social injustices of apartheid before being released and becoming president of his country.

Regardless of whether we relate to Sisyphus or Mandela, no one enjoys suffering that seems to go on indefinitely. And yet, our uncertainty about the duration of seasons of pain only compounds our distress. Day after day, week after week, months into years, we want our pain to cease, and we also want to understand its place in the purpose of our lives.

1) How long has your longest season of suffering lasted? Is it still ongoing, or has it ended? How did you endure the time spent suffering without knowing when it might end?

---

2) What person in the Bible, mythology, or history do you identify with when it comes to suffering? How does this person's story encourage you and give you strength to keep going in the midst of your own pain and turmoil?

_____

_____

_____

_____

It may be hard to comprehend that God uses what we consider to be painful seasons of suffering to fulfill the potential He has placed within us. As a result, we often fight against God's sovereignty because we dislike where His process has placed us. In our anger and pain, we may grow to distrust Him and pull away from His presence in our lives.

During these times that seem to go on forever, though, we must realize that they are only for a short duration within the scope of eternity. We're all being cultivated by the Master Vinedresser, and our growth takes time and usually costs us the comfort of everything we consider comfortable and familiar. We can't understand that God is up to His higher purposes because we feel so immersed in the trauma of our immediate circumstances.

God is intentional, however, in how He relocates the wild seeds of our lives and moves them into fields of promise we may not recognize as such. But every farmer knows that in order to remain fertile, soil must be upturned or it will go fallow, depleted of its nutrients and minerals and unable to accommodate new growth. We must accept that what feels like the unexpected event turning us upside down is really God making sure that we can continue to grow.

1) How have the crushing moments in your life had a domino effect in other areas of your life? How does one crisis in one area soon ripple into all dimensions of your being—work, home, family, relationships, and church?

_____

_____

_____

_____

2) Looking back, has your perspective changed on certain events that seemed crushing at the time? What has made the difference as you consider them now? How has God used those times as fertilizer for fueling your forward progress?

_____

_____

_____

_____

When we're concentrating on surviving the brutal blows of life, we often miss what God is doing through those moments. Like a master sculptor chipping away at the jagged edges of marble that interfere with the masterpiece He envisions, we must learn to realize that, as painful as each blow might be, they will not destroy us. We may come to see them, in fact, as necessary ingredients in the foundation of our maturation.

Fortunately, God doesn't expect us to understand or require us to comprehend His process in order for us to grow. He only expects your trust as you push through those dark and dirty places when you feel crushed by loss, betrayal, and heartache. It's when we're unwilling to trust Him and His purposes that we get in our own way and impede our progress. The reality is that we are never totally in control of events in our lives. Simply put, we can either place our faith in God or struggle in our own efforts without hope.

1) Before reading _Crushing_ and beginning this study guide, have you seriously considered that all the suffering in your life is necessary for your growth? Prior to beginning your encounter with these ideas in your present experience, how has God prepared you to see His fingerprints in times of past grief, physical injury, emotional loss, and overwhelming fear?

_____

_____

_____

_____

2) As you think back on your life and all the events, highs and lows and everything in between, that have brought you to this point in your life, can you see any kind of pattern forming? What does it look like? What would you compare it with?

_____

_____

_____

_____

3) What symbol, image, or scene comes to mind to describe how you presently view past suffering in your own life? Feel free to sketch, draw, or doodle your response as well as use words.

_____

_____

_____

_____

In order to maximize our momentum and make the most of our opportunities for growth, we must be willing to believe our pain is for a greater purpose. This truth means we must release whatever burdens of guilt, shame, and regret we may be carrying with us. Every bad decision, wasted moment of possible potential, lost relationship, and failed business must be unloaded from the weight you carry. Instead of allowing them to define you in defeat, disaster, and desperation, you must be willing to see them as God's building blocks for your best life ahead.

How can you do this? By having a heart-to-heart conversation with God about each and every one of those burdens. You have to realize the truth of your present situation: God would not have brought you to the place where you are right now, reading these words on this page, in order to abandon you now. He doesn't expect you to fulfill the potential for greatness He's placed within you by your own effort, hard work, and tenacity. He only wants you to lean into Him and change the way you view what you've been through and what you may go through in events yet to come.

1) If a stranger looked at you on an average day this past week, what would she have seen? What would you be wearing? How would accessories be a part of your ensemble? How would your countenance and demeanor look as a first impression to this stranger? Would she be able to guess your struggles and challenges just by looking at you? Or would she assume you have relatively few problems because of the veneer you keep in place most of the time?

_____

_____

_____

_____

2) What do you want others to see when they look at you right now? How can you balance healthy humility with Christ-centered confidence? How do you display your authentic self without leaving yourself open to being exploited or manipulated by others?

_____

_____

_____

_____

3) What burdens are you currently carrying? As quickly as possible, jot down at least ten items that are presently worrying you, disturbing your peace, or causing you stress.

_____

_____

_____

_____

4) Going back over your list of burdens, spend a few seconds lifting them before God in prayer. Take a deep breath in and then release a deep breath out in between praying and releasing each burden. Imagine that as you exhale, your burden is being handed over from you to God.

It's so tempting to waste valuable time and energy daring to think we know better than God—even as we struggle to make any kind of meaning out of the circumstances with which we presently struggle. Instead, be willing to dare stepping out in faith as we claim the promise of God's Word: "For I know the plans I have for you," declares the Lord, "plans to prosper you and not harm you, plans to give you hope and a future" (Jer. 29:11).

It may be hard to believe, especially when our losses add up over the years to a cumulative total greater than any single one of them. But the presence of pain in your life does not signal your demise. Rather, your crises and calamities are raw material for the masterpiece the Potter is shaping from your life.

You can review your most excruciating moments and know that they are not for nothing. No matter how atrocious, audacious, or heinous, God can heal the most horrific injuries and redeem the most shattering mistakes. But you must let Him in. You must trust that your Heavenly Father hasn't transplanted you and invested all the time and energy into growing you only to turn around and abandon you. You have to believe that you are exactly where He wants you because of where He wants to take you.

1) What is the basis for your faith? Be as unflinchingly honest as you can be and reflect on why you trust God at this point in your life. How much of your faith is based on what you inherited from others—family, friends, neighbors—versus what you have worked out in fear and trembling for yourself?

_____

_____

_____

_____

2) God's Word says, "Very truly I tell you, unless a kernel of wheat falls to the ground and dies, it remains only a single seed. But if it dies, it produces many seeds" (John 12:24). What needs to die in your life right now in order for new life to emerge? What are you reluctant to hand over to God but know in your heart needs to be surrendered?

_____

_____

_____

_____

3) Do you have any ideas about how God might use your past crushing seasons to make you stronger? Have you seen any benefits that He has already used or cultivated?

_____

_____

_____

_____

4) How have your dreams changed from when you were a teenager? What dreams have you given up on? Which ones do you still pursue and believe will come to pass? *How might God be using your past moments of crushing to fulfill your dreams?*

_____

_____

_____

_____

CHAPTER 4

Pruning Is Not Punishment

When it comes to life's crushing moments, perhaps none are more painful than those involving the health of our loved ones. When my young adult son Jamar suffered not one but two heart attacks in rapid succession, I was in Nigeria to preach at the invitation of a church there. Flying back on the long overseas trip home, I prayed desperately for God to spare his life and to heal his heart. I was blessed to see the Lord answer my prayers, which were also the prayers of so many family and friends, sooner rather than later.

Nonetheless, dealing with such an unexpected brush with death forced me once again to consider God's purpose in allowing such a harrowing experience. I truly believe that everything happens for a reason, even something as terrifying and traumatic as my son's heart attacks. But during those interminable moments of sitting and waiting in the cold, sterile corridor of the hospital, I couldn't help but feel like I was being punished.

1) What unexpected trauma or medical emergency comes to mind in your own experience that has left you feeling crushed at the time? How long ago was this crushing event? How has its consequences left an impact on you since then?

_____

_____

_____

_____

2) What was required of you in the midst of this crisis? How were you able to support loved ones and show them your support? Or how did they minister to you with their love, support, and encouragement?

_____

_____

_____

_____

3) How are you a different person now as a result of this experience? Why?

_____

_____

_____

_____

Our suffering during the crushing experiences of life, however, are not God's punishment. Even though they might feel just as painful, there's a crucial difference between pruning and punishment: intention. We shouldn't try to figure out how we suffer something but why. What possible purpose could such unbearable moments have in God's purpose for our life?

I believe the answer lies in the way God maintains control even as we wonder, from our limited viewpoint, why He is not exercising control in the way we would like. Instead, our life events in those dramatic times of devastation often feel totally out of our control, and we might even wonder if they're out of God's.

But nothing is beyond God's power, authority, and sovereignty. He knows what He's doing even when we can't fathom what possible good might come from a painful event.

You see, God doesn't cut us to kill us but to heal us. Consider the distinct difference between encountering a knife blade from the hands of a mugger in the inner city as compared with experiencing a surgeon's scalpel in an operating room.

On one hand, suffering a knife wound in a mugging could lead to infection, permanent disability, and death. The surgeon's cuts, however, alleviate pain, restore functioning, and facilitate healing of a larger problem. The pain of each may feel the same in the moment, but the intended outcome is vastly different.

1) During times of crushing disappointments, trials, and losses, have you ever felt like God was punishing you? Why did you feel this way? Did others contribute? If so, how?

_____

_____

_____

_____

2) What has given you strength and comfort during the hardest moments of your life? Or do you feel like you have just had to grit and grind your way through those times without any help whatsoever?

_____

_____

_____

_____

3) Do you agree that intentionality makes the difference between punishment and pruning? Why or why not?

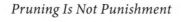

_____

_____

_____

_____

Depending on how we view God's intention in allowing us to suffer, we then determine how we perceive our pain. Even when we know that we must go through hard times in order for the seeds of our greatness to sprout into fruition, we will still struggle at times with feeling like we're being destroyed. If you think about it, being planted and being buried may feel similar if not identical—yet they each lead to incredibly different consequences.

In order to mature and ripen from our crushing blows, we must pay attention to how we perceive our suffering. Without denying or suppressing our pain and its expression, we must cling to the hope we have by faith in God. Like a tree being pruned by a master gardener, we are being cut only so we can grow stronger and straighter, taller and truer. We see this kind of response in a man whose name has become synonymous with suffering: Job. He expresses his truth while at the same time holding fast to his trust in the Lord:

> Keep silent and let me speak;
> then let come to me what may.
>> Why do I put myself in jeopardy
> and take my life in my hands?
>> Though he slay me, yet will I hope in him;
> I will surely defend my ways to his face.
>> Indeed, this will turn out for my deliverance,
> for no godless person would dare come before him! (Job 13:13–16)

Job's example reinforces what I have observed in the grief of others. Those individuals and families who express their anguish honestly and openly, without abandoning their faith, tend to heal more fully than others who try to pretend they're doing fine. Considering the magnitude of all Job lost, there's no way he could pretend to be doing fine. Nevertheless, he adamantly would not give up on God.

Perhaps Job understood that God allows such pruning just as a loving father disciplines a child so that the child will mature and reach her full potential. The Bible cautions us, "Do not despise the LORD's discipline, and do not resent his rebuke, because the LORD disciplines those he loves, as a father the son he delights in" (Prov. 3:11–12).

1) What did you learn about suffering from your parents, siblings, and other family members while you were growing up? What lessons did you absorb about what it means to endure pain?

_____

_____

_____

_____

2) How have your times of crushing been reflected in your faith and how you relate to God? Have there been times you have moved away from Him or given up your faith? Where are you with God at this point in your life?

_____

_____

_____

_____

3) How well do you express painful emotions during seasons of crushing? Do you tend to keep feelings bottled up until they explode? Or do you consistently share what you're feeling no matter how raw it may be?

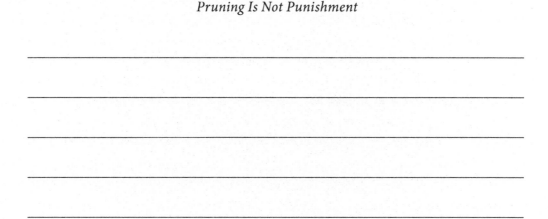

Sometimes I wonder if we learn the most—about life, about ourselves, about relationships, about love, about God—during life's most challenging moments. Because when our world falls apart and we're confronted by a crisis or catastrophe, then our priorities come into sharp focus. We have no time for what is unnecessary, trivial, and superfluous. We suddenly see what matters most, and we focus accordingly.

In my own life, after times of harvest I've often experienced times of pruning. Although these times still catch me by surprise, I know that the two often work hand in hand for God's larger purposes. His pruning of the branches of blessings in my life on the heels of a massive harvest reinforce what Jesus Himself told us: "Every branch in Me that does not bear fruit He takes away; And every *branch* that bears fruit He prunes, that it may bear more fruit" (John 15:2 NKJV).

As a result I've changed the way I view those times of pruning. I will never enjoy the pain of loss, uncertainty, and frustration in the moment. But I've learned to recognize that God is not pruning me because I've done something wrong. On the contrary, He is pruning me because I'm bearing fruit.

The same is true for you. If you are experiencing crushing moments in your life, then assume God wants to increase your harvest by pruning you back now so that you will produce more fruit later. At such times, you have been chosen by the Vinedresser to be pruned because you've done something that other branches have not: fulfilled your purpose by bearing fruit.

1) Can you think of a time in your life that now, looking back, you realize was God pruning you? How did you feel at the time it was happening? What makes the difference now that you didn't have then?

_____

_____

_____

_____

2) When crushing events occur in your life, what tends to be your initial reaction or default attitude? Do you automatically feel angry? Scared? Defeated? Or are you inclined to have a more positive, even hopeful response?

_____

_____

_____

_____

3) What kind of response would you like to have when hard things happen? What does it look like for you to express your pain while still keeping your faith in God?

_____

_____

_____

_____

During those times when we're being pruned by God, we still have a choice about how we respond. And it's not easy. We're experiencing the inescapable trauma of God cutting away many of the things in life we value most. In addition, the enemy of our souls often uses our desire for comfort to tempt us away from God's higher purpose for our lives.

Despite how you may feel in the moment, I urge you to keep in mind that nothing you lose is more valuable than what God wants to give you in its place. God does not value our material possessions and human achievements the way we do. Instead, He cherishes the eternal gifts being unlocked inside us as we look beyond our pleasure in this life. He likes taking what we view as the remnants and turning them into His Rembrandts.

Remember: your miracle is never in what you lost—it's in what you have left. You're not being punished by life's crushing seasons; you're being pruned for more productivity. Pruning is not punishment.

1) What have you lost that you continue to hold against God? A loved one? A relationship? A job or career? Material possessions? Something else?

_____

_____

_____

_____

2) What do the things you've lost represent to you? In what ways did they provide you with feeling that you are loved, secure, successful, or special?

_____

_____

_____

_____

3) What do you need to lay before God before you continue in this process of gaining a new perspective on crushing? Write them below and then spend a few minutes in prayer, trusting that you no longer have to carry them.

_____

_____

_____

_____

CHAPTER 5

Blood of the Vine

During a recent family gathering, I struggled to enjoy our festivities because I realized how many other families suffered. When times are good, it's tempting to overlook those who suffer in silence around us. Those who endure crushing, however, have their pain intensified when they are forgotten or overlooked by those celebrating around them.

Some holidays leave us with these same mixed emotions. We enjoy celebrating and count our blessings even as we grieve for and remember loved ones we have lost. We try to move on, but the suffering of others reminds us of our own losses. We know that regardless of our individual circumstances at any given moment, we all experience crushing moments that force us to confront our own painful losses. Our humanity unites us along with a desire to see our suffering produce change.

1) When have you been celebrating a holiday or other festive gathering and experienced a wave of sadness or memories of past crushing? How did you handle the tension between the two?

_____

_____

_____

_____

2) What has helped you get through holidays and anniversary dates following a season of mourning? What helps you now as you experience the bittersweet collision of past and present?

_____

_____

_____

_____

3) How does being with other people—family, friends, church community—make it easier to endure these times of celebration shadowed by loss or pain? How does being with other people at these times make it harder for you? Why?

_____

_____

_____

_____

The words *testify* and *testament* both have the same Latin root word, *testi*, literally meaning "witness." In the Bible both these words are tied to the significance of blood and the importance God places on it. In Scripture we see how blood becomes a way to give life, to communicate, to reveal, to protect, to seal, to atone, and to save.

In the Old Testament, the blood of slaughtered lambs shed on the altars in the temple became the means of atonement for people's sins prior to Christ's death on the cross, which emerges in the New Testament. The contrast between these two sacrifices is important because one was temporary—the bloodshed of animals for that moment's sacrifice—and the other eternal as Jesus' shed blood and resurrection forever defeated sin and death.

We also see this contrast in the central theme of each canon. The Old Testament bears witness to the fall of mankind because the stain of human sin is transferred from generation to generation by blood. On the other hand, the New Testament testifies of the redemption of mankind through the eternal blood of Jesus Christ, transferred from person to person by accepting His sacrifice on their behalf.

1) When was the last time you bled or saw your own blood? How did it make you feel when you saw it? Why?

_____

_____

_____

_____

2) Why do you believe blood was such an important part of sacrificial offerings in the Old Testament?

_____

_____

_____

_____

3) How does blood "testify" to what is true about who we are as human beings? As God's children created in His image?

_____

_____

_____

_____

Jesus serves as the perfect example of how crushing leads to resurrection and transformation. First, God sent His only Son into our world to be born in a manger to a poor carpenter and his virgin bride. Jesus grew into a man who revealed Himself to be the Messiah. He healed the sick, fed the multitudes, walked on water, hung out with outcasts, and forgave sinners. But that was just the beginning of why He came.

The crushing Christ endured goes beyond any suffering we can imagine. He was crushed in every way—physically beaten, emotionally isolated, and spiritually bereft. After being whipped by soldiers, Jesus carried His own cross before His body was nailed to its wooden, rough-hewn surface. Excruciating pain must have electrified every nerve in His body. Even as nails in His hands became unbearable, He shifted His weight only to feel more pain from the iron spikes pinning His ankles.

Christ's physical trauma reflected the emotional and spiritual distress within. We can assume that because our emotions are given to us by our Creator, and because we are made in His image, then He experiences His own kind of emotions. The Bible tells us that Jesus experienced everything known to the human condition—joy, sorrow, anger—without allowing any emotion to become an entrance for sin. With His Father forsaking Him in order that He might die only to rise again and save all of humankind, Christ experienced an utter loneliness and isolation that we will never fully comprehend.

Jesus endured all of this crushing only so we could be reconnected, restored, and redeemed for relationship with God. Christ's suffering served the greatest purpose possible. He reminds us that our pain is never in vain.

1) How did the blood offerings of the Old Testament change in the New Testament? In other words, why did Christ have to shed His blood and die in order to pay for our sins?

_____

_____

_____

_____

2) What feelings arise in you as you consider the suffering Jesus endured for your sake on the cross? How do these emotions affect your relationship with Him? Why?

_____

_____

_____

_____

3) What emotions within you do you struggle to identify in Christ? Anger? Disappointment? Loneliness? Something else? Why do you have a difficult time imagining that Jesus felt this way?

_____

_____

_____

_____

When we're faced with the bloody trauma of crushing, we often feel we have no choice but to accept death and move on. In order to survive, we pronounce certain areas of our life dead and bury it deep within us. We carry these ashes of our dreams within us, part of the bitter burden that lingers in the wake of life's crushing events.

Christ's resurrection from the grave, however, forces us to reconsider the purpose of all that we have buried in our lives. What was once tainted by the inadequacy of our own effort and sinful failures can be resurrected and used as a reflection of our Savior's power and God's glory. Jesus did not die just to save you—he died for every part of us that we have ever given up on and abandoned. We can know life through the resurrection power of the Lord stepping out of the darkness of the tomb.

1) What dreams have died within you since your adolescence? What has been the cause of their expiration? Which ones' ashes do you still carry inside you?

_____

_____

_____

_____

_____

2) How often do you think about dreams that you believe are no longer attainable? How do you feel when they come to mind?

_____

_____

_____

_____

_____

3) What dream have you refused to let die inside you, despite all the crushing moments of your life? How have you kept it alive all these years? What do you need to do next to breathe life into it?

_____

_____

_____

_____

_____

Crushing grapes not only expresses the juice from the skins containing the fruit, but it also separates the unusable parts of the grape from the juice. If grapes are not picked when ripened, they dry up and the branch loses strength to remain connected to the vine. The fruit falls and rots on the ground, never to be transformed into the exquisite wine it might have been.

As our Master Vintner, God wants to save us from dying on the vine or rotting on the ground. He wants us to let go of the fruit of past seasons' harvest in order to discover the fruit we will become—and better still, the eternal wine He wants to make from all the fruit within us. We must let go of the fruit we've lost as well as the fruit that we cling to as our greatest achievements. Instead, we must choose to celebrate the suffering that comes with crushing in order to become divine wine served for His purposes.

1) What are you looking forward to in your life that has not yet come about—for instance, changing careers, getting married, or starting a family? What are you presently doing to facilitate this anticipated goal?

_____

_____

_____

_____

2) When was the last time you shared your dreams with God and asked His blessing and favor over them? Take a few minutes now and list at least three big goals you want to fulfill with God's help.

_____

_____

_____

_____

CHAPTER 6

The Price of Crushing

How many times have you thought, *If only I knew then what I know now!* While I value all that God has done in my life and continues to do, if He had allowed me to see all the crushing moments of my life up front, I would never have made it through them. My fears and doubts would have only compounded my anxiety as I awaited each of those seasons of crushing. Fortunately, God does not reveal everything in our life to us at the beginning. Instead, He asks us to rely on Him step by step, one day at a time.

I realize that not knowing also presents challenges that seem to add to the impact of our crushing. We feel blindsided, caught off guard, and hijacked by events so unexpected they take our breath away. Yet, if we had known what was going to hit us and when it would land, then we would have likely taken flight. God knows us intimately, however, and does not want us to settle for mediocre lives. He wants to use those times that feel unbearable to make us stronger.

1) What decision, situation, or relationship do you sometimes wish you could do over? Why? How would you act or choose differently if given the chance to do it again?

_____

_____

_____

_____

2) How has God shown you that it's sometimes a blessing not to get what you ask for? How has this awareness changed the way you pray? Why?

_____

_____

_____

_____

3) When have you most recently felt like you were settling for less than God's best in some area of your life? What were the circumstances around this occasion? Do you still feel that way? Why or why not?

_____

_____

_____

_____

Like many of us, the people of Israel also seemed to prefer having a mediocre life rather than go through the wilderness to get to the Promised Land. Although they had been enslaved in Egypt for many generations and had been crying out to God to deliver them, when He finally began to lead them to their new home, they tended to hate the journey. They wanted instant gratification, feeling justified in rebelling against God at times in order to pursue the pleasures and comforts they believed were their due.

But God had a larger plan in place. After the Hebrew people had been led out of Egypt by Moses, after they had passed through the symbolically cleansing waters of the Red Sea, God allowed them to wander in the desert. Along the way, however, He instructed Moses to build the first tabernacle erected as God's sacred dwelling. The Lord's instructions were quite detailed and required that His house be constructed according to His specific design (Exod. 25:40).

Clearly, God had something special in mind by providing such a unique blueprint for the place where His people would worship Him. Moses' tabernacle, as it was called, was also known as the tent of meeting and included three sections: the outer court, the inner court or Holy Place, and the Most Holy Place or Holy of Holies. The three features that people encountered when first entering the tabernacle—mirrors, water, and a fiery altar—were especially symbolic. They reminded priests as well as pilgrims to look within themselves and to cleanse and purify their hearts before offering their sacrifices of atonement.

1) When have you looked back on your life at a time that felt painful or difficult in the moment but now feels better?

_____

_____

_____

_____

2) How do past mistakes and times of crushing influence the way you make major decisions in your life? Do you consider yourself more of a risk taker or safety seeker? Why?

_____

_____

_____

_____

3) What intrigues you most about the very specific design God gave to Moses for the tabernacle in Exodus 25:40? How does this aspect resonate within your own life presently?

_____

_____

_____

_____

These three symbolic stages also parallel the first three steps in the process of wine-making. Grapes are plucked in the vineyard and brought to the winepress, where they would be trampled and crushed in order to release their juices. Then the juice from the grapes would flow into a storage vat, but not before passing through a filter to strain impurities and pulp from the liquid.

Similarly, our crushing coincides with the initial sacrifice that would take place when the Israelites entered the tent of meeting. They would sacrifice an unblemished animal, often a lamb, on the brazen altar to atone for their sins. Instead of their own blood being shed under sin's penalty of death, the animal took their place. The temple priests, after examining and washing themselves, would enter in to the inner court, the Holy Place, in order to accept the sacrifice and forgive the supplicant on God's behalf.

While Jesus became the ultimate Lamb of God sacrificed for all our sins once and for all, we still cannot escape the necessity of our own crushing, washing, and reflection as part of the process.

1) What have you had to sacrifice in the past in order to follow Christ? How did you feel at the time about giving up these items, relationships, or habits? Now how do you feel about what you sacrificed?

_____

_____

_____

_____

2) How often do you reflect on your life and ask God to forgive you for recent transgressions? How frequently do you confess to others?

_____

_____

_____

_____

3) When was the last time you asked someone to forgive you for offending them in some way? What consequences emerged from your apology?

_____

_____

_____

_____

Considering the pattern we see in the construction and utilization of Moses' tabernacle, which is the same essential pattern we find in the process of making wine, we should not be surprised to realize that this pattern reached its perfection in the life, death, and resurrection of Jesus. He did for us what we could not do for ourselves. He experienced the ultimate crushing so that we might become God's ultimate wine.

In order to become God's wine, though, we cannot escape our crushing. I often marvel at how people erroneously believe that accepting Christ into their lives results in an elimination of pain from their lives. We know, in fact, that just the opposite is true. Jesus said, "I have told you these things, so that in me you may have peace. In this world you will have trouble. But take heart! I have overcome the world" (John 16:33).

Considering what we see in the Bible, in both the Old and New Testaments, the first thing we should expect when we begin our relationship with God is to encounter trouble.

It's not that God is a sadist and wants us to suffer. It's simply that there is a price that must be paid in order for us to appreciate and value what we have been so freely given. While the Lord so freely gives us His abundant blessings, He never promised that we would escape suffering as we experience them. Crushing is the price we pay to become all that God created us to be.

1) What item have you purchased that required you to save for a long time in order to acquire it? Your home? A new car? A beautiful coat or piece of jewelry? A precious gift for a loved one? How did having to save over time in order to purchase this item affect the way you perceived its value?

_____

_____

_____

_____

2) What are you willing to pay in order to experience the fullness of being who God made you to be? What's the hardest part of paying this price? Why?

_____

_____

_____

_____

3) Think back to when you first began your personal relationship with God. What did you expect at that time? What would you tell yourself, knowing what you know and being who you are presently, if you could go back to that moment now?

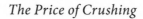

_____

_____

_____

_____

While we can pursue meaning, purpose, and pleasure in many ways in this life, none satisfy us like knowing God and fulfilling the divine destiny He has for us. As part of this process of knowing Him and growing into the likeness of His perfect Son, Jesus Christ, we are called to encounter just a small degree of His suffering as the price. Consequently, our Master Vintner uses our life's struggles, strife, and suffering to refine us into His masterpiece.

With this knowledge of how God uses crushing in our lives, we should be willing to run toward it instead of away from it as we often do. In the Bible we're told, "Consider it pure joy, my brothers and sisters, whenever you face trials of many kinds, because you know that the testing of your faith produces perseverance. Let perseverance finish its work so that you may be mature and complete, not lacking anything" (James 1:2–4).

We shouldn't be surprised and despair when we feel crushed—it's simply the onset of spiritual growing pains.

Similar to precursors such as Israel's crushing enslavement in Egypt and then their crushing sacrifices at the brazen altar in Moses' tabernacle, Christ's crushing death on the cross was necessary for our transformation. We, too, must be willing to endure crushing in order to release what God has placed inside us. He invites us to His winepress so that He can do with us that which is necessary to reconnect something temporal to its eternal source.

Your crushing is simply the beginning of a glorious transformation process that will reveal who God made you to be. Crushing releases all the gifts, talents, strengths, and abilities within you even as it removes the veneers you may be using to hide from pain.

Crushing is not going to last and, like the labor pains of an expectant mother, will produce new life.

1) Have you ever had a moment when something painful, difficult, or challenging occurred and you immediately thanked God and "considered it joy"? If so, what difference did this response make in you? If not, then what prevents you from having this kind of response?

_____

_____

_____

_____

2) Just as it's necessary for a business owner to take inventory in order to know the contents and value of their business, it can sometimes be helpful to take stock of the major assets and liabilities in your life emotionally and spiritually. Complete the following brief inventory by filling in the blanks.

Some of the best moments in my life include _____,

_____, and _____.

The hardest times that have crushed me would be _____,

_____, and _____.

A major turning point for the better in my life occurred when _____

_____.

A major crushing moment that left me wrecked was when _____

_____.

3) What large pattern or major theme do you see running continuously throughout your life? Before you answer, consider which genre you would use to best describe your life so far from the list below. You may circle all that apply, but try to choose only one.

Reality TV show competition
Romance novel
Improv comedy

Driver's education test
Old Western movie
Soap opera
Broadway musical
Tragic opera
Situation comedy (sitcom)
Horror movie
Superhero comic book
Ancient history text
Something else:

What title would you give your story based on the genre you chose? Why?

_____

_____

_____

_____

CHAPTER 7

Let's Make Wine

When I was trying to build the church God had called me to build, I experienced people who had no knowledge of who I was or what our congregation was like tell me that what we wanted to do could not be done. They tried to deny our construction loan, ignore our requests for meetings, and lose us on an endless paper trail of forms. But with each rejection, I only grew stronger in my resolve. I knew I was doing what God had anointed me to do, and I knew without a doubt He would provide the resources in His timing.

In the process of your crushing, the enemy of your soul will send obstacles your way in order to derail, distract, and disrupt what God is doing in your life. Roadblocks you could not imagine will spring out of nowhere. Family, friends, and coworkers will inevitably surprise you, fail you, betray you. Problems and pressures you didn't know existed will come to life and consume your attention, time, and energy.

You can toss and turn every night, you can fall to the ground as your knees buckle, and you can cry out to God again and again. But these temptations, trials, and tragedies cannot deter the process of crushing God wants to use in your life—unless you let them.

1) What obstacles have you faced in pursuit of the dream you knew God had called you to fulfill? How did you respond to them?

_____

_____

_____

_____

2) What temptations, setbacks, and speed bumps have you encountered most recently as you try to follow God and grow closer to Him (perhaps even after beginning this study)?

_____

_____

_____

_____

3) On a scale of 1 to 10, with 1 being completely unwilling and 10 being total surrender, how willing are you to embrace your crushing like Job, who lost everything but still said, "Though He slay me, yet will I trust Him" (Job 13:15, NKJV)?

_____

_____

_____

_____

As an entrepreneur, I'm often asked variations of the same question over and over again: Is the painful price of launching my dream worth it? Some ask about the easiest methods or the quickest shortcuts. Others want to know how they can reap the greatest profit with the least amount of investment. My answer to these individuals reflects the message at the heart of *Crushing*. What God wants to do in your life will cost you everything.

The late, great evangelist Kathryn Kuhlman preached a sermon once in which she shared what it had cost her to be who God had called her to be. She said that it cost her everything, and I've never forgotten her raw honesty and truthful candor. From my own experience, this is certainly the case.

The crushing process in your life will cost you everything you know about yourself, everything you think you want, and everything you understand about those around you. But through this process, you will go from the breast milk beliefs required by new-borns to the meat-and-potatoes faith that will sustain you in your maturation. God will take the food of your failures and transform it into a banquet of blessings. He wants to shift your seedpod mindset into the ripening attitude of fruit willing to be crushed in order to make wine. This decision on your part is not a one-time event—it's a daily choice that affects how you see everything that happens to you.

1) How do you feel as you consider that the cost of your crushing is everything you have? Do you agree that this is the price for your transformation into God's wine? Why or why not?

_____

_____

_____

_____

2) What single event, good or bad, has had the greatest impact on your faith? Why?

_____

_____

_____

_____

3) Do you consider yourself a mature person spiritually? Why or why not? How would you define spiritual maturity in your own life? What would it look like?

_____

_____

_____

_____

4) Are you willing to keep trusting God in the midst of crushing pain? Are you willing to sacrifice the time it takes to be your best? Will you sacrifice what is good in your life in order to achieve the greatness latent within you?

_____

_____

_____

_____

The night before His death, Jesus and His disciples met to eat the Passover meal together. During this time together, Jesus used common elements on their table—bread and wine—to create a timeless symbolic ritual that we still celebrate today. From that Passover table, we find the tipping point of our salvation. Jesus was about to pay the price of our salvation on the cross, and He wanted His followers to forever commemorate His broken body and shed blood by partaking of the communion we usually now call the Lord's Supper. Jesus paid everything and invites us to do the same if we want to follow Him.

Christ not only paid the ultimate price for our salvation, but He also paid for our transformation. He set the example of what it looks like to embrace crushing in order to release the sweet fragrance of the Holy Spirit in our lives. He shows us what it costs to love completely and sacrificially. He said that others would know us by our love.

Our Heavenly Father knows all about the price of sacrificial love because He was willing to give up His only Son so that we could all be reunited in relationship with Him. We might have a tiny grasp on understanding the price of pain in the midst of our crushing, but God has already made the ultimate sacrifice. In addition, He continues to provide protection and provision like any loving parent wants to give to their children.

1) Putting aside what you've heard or read about the Lord's Supper, why do you think Jesus took the bread and wine and told His disciples to eat and drink His body and blood?

_____

_____

_____

_____

2) How important is it to continue observing the Lord's Supper, communion, as part of your worship community? What does it mean to you personally?

_____

_____

_____

_____

Every successful person I know carries the scars and bruises of their crushing. So many people try to change the world, launch a business, or start a new ministry but refuse to let anyone glimpse the price of pain they have paid for their endeavor. Personally, however, I don't consider anyone credible if they aren't willing to celebrate the battle scars that led to their ongoing victory. Perhaps this explains why Jesus had to be the first spiritual fruit crushed into eternal wine.

Christ endured the shame of the cross for the joy set before Him (Heb. 12:2). This sacred joy blossomed from the shame of the cross and became the fruit of the church, His bride, which could not have existed without His sacrifice. All the suffering, anguish, humiliation, shame, and pain were required in order for His beloved bride to be set free. He took all the crushing upon Him so that it could become something forever potent and powerful.

Through His loving example, we can take the juice of our journey and make wine. No matter what we've lost, how much money we've wasted, how many relationships have fallen apart, or how many tears we have shed—let's make wine!

1) What scars, wounds, or bruises do you have on your soul from your life's crushing moments? What baggage do you carry with you from all the pain you've endured?

_____

_____

_____

_____

2) What trophies, mementos, or souvenirs of God's grace do you carry with you? These might be tangible items, such as a cross or a loved one's Bible, or something intangible.

_____

_____

_____

_____

3) Looking at your responses to questions 1 and 2 above, is there any overlap? In other words, have some scars of crushing become reminders of grace?

_____

_____

_____

_____

4) What new opportunities have developed in your life from the vacant places of loss? How have you seen God begin to grow something new where you once experienced nothing but pain?

_____

_____

_____

_____

5) What's the biggest change you want God to bring about in your life right now? Why? What result do you expect to see when such a change occurs?

CHAPTER 8

Power in the Blood

Crushing for the purposes of making God's eternal wine requires us to change the way we see our lives. Just as winemaking necessitates that the grapes must be crushed to extract the juice for fermentation, our crushing relies on the power of blood to pay the price, which Jesus did for us on the cross. While God is certainly not violent or sadistic, He requires us to value the gift of grace we have been given.

Blood is the life force that brings oxygen, nutrients, and minerals to all parts of our bodies. Consequently, we see the way blood has always played a vital role in how we approach God. One of the most uncomfortable moments can be found when Moses, after conversing with God through the burning bush (Exod. 3:1–17), leaves Midian, along with his wife, Zipporah, and their children in order to confront Pharaoh with God's message:

> At a lodging place on the way, the LORD met Moses and was about to kill Him. But Zipporah took a flint knife, cut off her son's foreskin and touched Moses' feet with it. "Surely you are a bridegroom of blood to me," she said. So the LORD let him alone. (At that time she said "bridegroom of blood," referring to circumcision.)
>
> (Exod. 4:24–26)

1) What does blood symbolize to you? Why?

_____

_____

_____

_____

2) When you consider its importance in the Bible, which we've already started to explore, what strikes you about the way God values blood?

_____

_____

_____

_____

3) What stands out or speaks to you in this scene where Moses' wife obeys God and makes him a "bridegroom of blood"? What troubles you in this scene? And what makes sense to you?

_____

_____

_____

_____

This passage often troubles readers for many reasons. Why would an all-knowing, all-powerful God commission Moses to lead His people out of bondage in Egypt only to kill Moses before He even begins? We know God never goes back on His word. So why is circumcision apparently so significant to the Lord—so important that it becomes, literally, a matter of life and death for someone God Himself chose?

To answer these questions, we must remember how God has interacted with His people prior to this encounter. Specifically, we should recall how God went about making a promise to Abram that included changing, or revealing in a more authentic way, who God made Abram to be—symbolized by his new name, Abraham.

There's a nuanced difference between these two similar names that reveals the change taking place. *Abram* means "high/exalted father," while *Abraham* means "father of many nations." This name-changing, life-altering covenant God made with Abraham reflects the change God has relentlessly pursued ever since Adam and Eve sinned by disobeying God and eating the forbidden fruit from the Tree of the Knowledge of Good and Evil (Gen. 2:16–17). As a way of sealing this covenant with Abraham, God required him to cut away the foreskin from his penis, a powerful symbol of intimate surrender. Abraham received a new name and his physical body bore the scar that visibly and tangibly illustrated how he was set apart by God from all others.

1) If someone asked you why God required His people to be circumcised in ancient times, what would you tell them? How would you explain the spiritual significance of circumcision?

_____

_____

_____

_____

2) In light of how important circumcision functions symbolically to God, how do you regard the role of spiritual symbols in your own life?

_____

_____

_____

_____

3) What symbols or rituals carry powerful meaning for you in your relationship with God? Why?

_____

_____

_____

_____

When we fast-forward through Hebrew history for hundreds of years, we see Abraham's descendants—the ones God promised him in their covenant—enslaved in Egypt. In order to maintain their cultural and religious identity in a way distinct from their captors, the Jewish people continued the ritual of circumcision. Maintaining this ritual, even while they were in bondage, continually reminded them to keep their faith in God and to trust that He would one day deliver them.

Coming back to Moses and the life-saving emergency surgery his wife performs in the desert, we see that God is simply making sure His people continue to uphold their part of the covenant. Bottom line: How could Moses lead the rest of the Jewish people if he himself had not physically demonstrated his personal faith in God and God's promises?

As we endure crushing events, experiences, and exhaustion, we might do well to remember how God has always maintained His faithfulness to His people. Time after time, even when they wander away into idolatry and sinfulness, God always pursues those He loves and wants to know. With this in mind, we must consider the implications for our own soul-numbing, life-threatening moments. If God has always kept His promises to His people—Abraham, Moses, the nation of Israel, and on and on—then doesn't it make sense that He will keep His promises to us?

Keep in mind that God is passionately determined to save His children and restore relationship with them. Not only does He want to forgive us and give us a new identity—God also wants to rescue us, redeem us, and restore us. He wants us to know the joy, peace, and hope that comes from living purposefully, motivated by love and fueled by grace. Circumcision is no longer a physical requirement of our relationship with Him because of what Jesus did on the cross. But God still wants us to know the acute price that Jesus paid for us.

1) How does God sometimes remind you of what He's done for you in the past?

_____

_____

_____

_____

_____

2) What holidays, events, or symbols help you practice thanksgiving and give God praise for His presence and blessings in your life? What rituals or habits do you practice at these times?

_____

_____

_____

_____

3) When have you wandered from God because of the pain, stress, and anguish in your life? How did he pursue you despite your attempts to run?

_____

_____

_____

_____

Knowing God and being in relationship with Him forever changes our perspective on our life's darkest, most painful moments—but only when we realize the price we carry still for the privilege of free will. If we no longer have to be circumcised physically because of Jesus' death and resurrection, then why do we have to feel any pain at all in life? Because we still get to choose whether we will love and serve God. We can rebel and run away from Him, or we can suffer the price of our freedom and run to Him.

It's no coincidence, of course, that Jesus' name in Hebrew is Yeshua, which carries connotative meaning with words such as *salvation* and *protection*. Could it be that our crushing reminds us that we must choose to enter into a covenant with God? In the Garden of Eden, after Adam and Eve have sinned and were hiding from God, He took the life of an innocent animal and used its skin to cover Adam and Eve's nakedness (Gen. 3:21). Later, their son Abel brought to the Lord an acceptable sacrifice that consisted of fat portions from the firstborn of his flock (Gen. 4:4–5). Many generations after that, Moses follows God's instructions and commands the people of Israel to take a lamb without defect, eat it, and place its blood on the doorframes of each house (Exod. 12:1–13).

Time and again, God's signature points to the power of blood to seal our relationship with Him. On the cross, Jesus shed His blood—after symbolically asking His followers to partake of His suffering via bread and wine as His body and blood the night before. Rather than suffer spiritual death and spend eternity apart from God, we can now enjoy intimate fellowship because of what our Savior did for us. Christ became our sacrificial Lamb whose blood was spilled and smeared upon the doors of our hearts.

The bloodshed of God's Son saved your life. He spilled His blood on the cross to pay the debt of sin you could not pay. Jesus endured the ultimate crushing so that you could be free. Your crushing is not without purpose—God is always at work in the midst of it.

1) Thinking about the role that blood plays in most of the major stories in the Old Testament, which story speaks to your life right now? With which Bible personality do you most identify at this season of life? Why?

_____

_____

_____

_____

2) How has God stripped you of your defenses in order to help you grow stronger and become more mature?

_____

_____

_____

_____

3) What keeps you aware of the price that Jesus paid on the cross for your sins? How do you make sure His sacrifice maintains its power in your life instead of becoming too familiar as a sentimental cliché?

_____

_____

_____

_____

CHAPTER 9

A Vat Full of Wait

Despite our inability to see it at the time, we should thank God that He often makes us wait. Our culture is so focused on high-speed immediate gratification, but some things simply cannot be rushed. Winemaking, both literally and spiritually, takes time. We may think we're ready for what we want or what we've asked God to give us, but He knows we may not be ready to handle it yet even if He plans to give it to us.

Instead, we need to grow stronger, wiser, and sharper. During those seasons that follow our hardest moments, we have to learn patience. We can trust that as we rebuild, rediscover, and reorient ourselves to life after this latest blow, God is working on us. He is working on our character, our heart, and our mind. He is strengthening our determination and softening our stubbornness. He is instilling in us wisdom, discernment, and compassion. God has not brought us through the wilderness in order to leave us overwhelmed and underdeveloped.

Most people I know who have discovered the joyful contentment that comes from fulfilling their God-given purpose had to wait. I'm no exception, and neither are you. I ministered for seven years before I preached my first sermon, but during that time I still prepared hundreds of sermons. I was in a holding pattern but knew that God would eventually clear me for takeoff. You can trust that no matter how long you have been waiting, God will always be on time to deliver what you need next.

1) When have you endured a season where God clearly made you wait for something you wanted or prayed for? How did you handle it? Did it change your perspective on waiting? Why or why not?

_____

_____

_____

_____

2) Rank yourself on the following patience scale by circling the number and descriptor that best expresses how you usually respond when forced to wait:

1	2	3	4	5	6	7	8	9	10
calm	restless	anxious	nervous	edgy	frustrated	angry			

3) What are you waiting on God for right now? How long have you been waiting?

_____

_____

_____

_____

Waiting can be especially challenging when we allow our fears to eclipse our faith. Like survivors of an earthquake, we often experience the aftershock of our crushing crisis as consequences continue to shift the ground beneath us. We may feel anxious and edgy, wondering when the next wave will send us reeling. Try as we may to experience God's presence and to follow His voice, we struggle to feel connected to Him on a daily basis. In the midst of such ongoing misery, we continually confront our concerns about why God would allow us to go through such a dark valley of despair.

During these seasons of waiting and wondering, you have to be honest about all you're feeling and try to find constructive ways to express your anger, anxiety, and angst about your experience. At the very least, you can share your feelings without being destructive in how you reveal them. Be kind to yourself, just as a kind, loving parent would soothe and comfort a child. Allow the weather of your emotions to storm, but allow that storm to pass, knowing that the bedrock of your faith will always remain.

1) When have you been caught off guard by the aftershocks or consequences of a major crushing blow? How did the first assault trigger the ones that followed?

_____

_____

_____

_____

2) How do you maintain your faith when confronted by an unexpected disappointment, shocking loss, or unimaginable setback?

_____

_____

_____

_____

3) If interviewed and asked for a description of how you handle life's most painful moments, what would the following groups of people say about you?

Family:

_____

_____

_____

_____

Close friends:

_____

_____

_____

_____

Coworkers:

_____

_____

_____

_____

New acquaintances:

_____

_____

_____

_____

Church family:

_____

_____

_____

_____

So often, we feel the way we do in the midst of our crushing times because we've lost something we deem valuable, perhaps even irreplaceable. But to God, our Master Vintner, *we* are what is valuable and irreplaceable! Basically, we cling to what we do and what we achieve, while God is entirely focused on our character, our being. With this contrast in mind, I suspect that the very things we lose may, in fact, be obstacles to the true growth that God is cultivating in our souls.

Shifting to God's perspective, you are the fruit, not the product, of your labors or what you've accumulated or accomplished. Knowing that you are still growing, developing, ripening, and then fermenting, God continues to do whatever is necessary to produce His best wine from you, His fruit. You don't have to worry about what's ahead or what might occur if your worst fears are realized. God is with you. He always has been and He always will see you through, no matter how intensely you may suffer.

1) Generally, do you agree that what we lose in life's crushing moments clears the way for us to mature in our faith? Why or why not?

_____

_____

_____

_____

2) How have you experienced God developing your character and growing your faith most recently?

_____

_____

_____

_____

3) How often do you worry about what the future holds? What helps you cope with your fears, worries, concerns, and anxieties? What role does your faith play in your coping strategy?

_____

_____

_____

_____

During this season of waiting, the fermentation from your crushing begins taking place within you. While it might feel like nothing is really changing, you can trust that nothing will ever be the same as you become stronger, wiser, and more dependent on God as the source of your identity and power. From our fermentation, we become mature enough to handle more than we could before. We trust that God is in control so we don't have to worry about the ultimate outcome, no matter how painful the immediate moment may seem.

In winemaking, the fermentation stage is simply a waiting period for the grape juice to transform into alcohol. The fruit has been crushed so the essence of the grapes, their juice, is simply collected and stored. The invisible process of juice fermenting into wine takes place gradually, without dramatic trauma experienced when the grapes were pressed.

This season is when you may feel most despondent because you can't see any possible positive growth emerging from your pain. This is the time between when Jesus died and when He arose from the tomb, leaving it empty for the women to find on the morning of the third day. Similarly, a resurrection is happening within you, so don't lose heart simply because your tomb is not yet vacated by the new life God is returning to life within you. Keep in mind that the cliché about the night appearing darkest before the dawn often holds true. After all, the disciples did not know their Master would return from the dead until they saw Him, heard Him, and felt His touch.

1) What signs of positive growth have others told you they have seen in you following times of loss, disappointment, or pain? How did you feel when they told you?

_____

_____

_____

_____

2) What indications of fermentation can you spot in your life right now? Where do you see signs that you are growing stronger because of the crushing you've endured?

_____

_____

_____

_____

3) How do you think God is using your past times of pain to shape your future? Where do you see evidence of this transformation in your life?

_____

_____

_____

_____

Your fermentation period may feel just as painful as your crushing, even though the actual cause of your pain has subsided. But this period is actually just a time of transition. Your life is changing and will not always be in this in-between time that you may feel you're in. In many ways the hard work is over. Now, the Vintner only requires you to be patient. You've been crushed again and again. Your juice has been extracted. You can now trust that God's divine hand is upon you as you ferment into full potency and flavor.

Nothing in our culture will assist you in this endeavor of waiting. Others will not be able to give you the patience required to see your development fulfilled. You probably hate to wait as much as I do, but the reality is God's timing runs on total, eternal perfection.

So no matter what you do, don't you dare give up!

1) How have you grown stronger and more capable because you refused to give up on God?

_____

_____

_____

_____

2) Do you believe you are more patient, less patient, or about the same as you were ten years ago? One year ago? What accounts for the change? Or if you don't believe you've changed, how do you cope when forced to wait?

_____

_____

_____

_____

CHAPTER 10

Out of the Tomb and into the Bottle

As I share in chapter 10 of *Crushing*, my wife's recovery after an excruciating season of physical pain brought us great relief, because even though she continued to suffer, we knew that her body was healing. The pain began relenting more each day as she grew stronger. The destructive pain that threatened her health and robbed her peace was replaced by the constructive pain of healing and restoration.

If you've ever recovered from a serious injury or debilitating condition, then you know there's pain on both sides. First, you experience the growing discomfort that gradually—or sometimes quickly and dramatically—electrifies your body with acute nerve-shattering pain. Once the cause of the pain is identified and alleviated or removed, then your body begins the process of restoring what has been damaged, stressed, or lost.

This parallels the way we begin shifting our energies as we realize our crushing is now resulting in fermentation. We begin to glimpse what God is up to. We see a way forward. We feel the first sparks of hope flint from our faith forecast of the future.

1) When has your body suffered a disease, injury, or ailment that forced you to confront your physical limitations? How did you manage the pain involved? And how was the pain of recovery different?

_____

_____

_____

_____

2) Do you consider yourself to have a high tolerance for physical pain? Or is your sensitivity to pain in your body highly acute?

_____

_____

_____

_____

3) When you know that pain is making your body stronger, such as when you work out with weights, does this awareness motivate you to persevere? Why or why not?

_____

_____

_____

_____

When Jesus arose from the tomb, He left its vacancy as a relic of His resurrection. The women who ventured out that early morning found only a massive stone beside the gaping cavern of the burial chamber. Inside, they found only the crumpled burial shroud.

Strangely enough, however, it was not the empty tomb that became the major symbol of Jesus' followers in the early church. Instead, they eventually chose the instrument of their Savior's death, the cross. In many ways, this was an odd and chilling reminder, because the cross was well known as the common way to execute criminals in one of the most painful ways possible. In Jesus' time, the cross carried the same kinds of connotations we might associate with lethal injection, the electric chair, or the gas chamber.

While we now use the cross as a symbol of worship and recognize its eternal significance, we must be careful not to lose sight of its original impact. The crushing power of the cross was both physical as well as spiritual. We now celebrate the cross only because Jesus was not defeated by it. As a result, the cross reminds us of God's life-giving, death-defying power to bring His eternal wine out of our momentary pain.

1) What's your immediate reaction when you see a cross in our culture today? Does it make a difference whether you see a cross on a church or around the neck of a young teen on the street? Why?

_____

_____

_____

_____

2) What does the cross mean to you at this point in your life? In what ways has it become too familiar and lost its meaning? How do you keep it personally relevant?

_____

_____

_____

_____

For over a month, Jesus revealed Himself among His followers in various times, places, and points of contact, making sure that those who loved Him realized that the crushing devastation they shared when He was killed was now overshadowed by the joy of His return. Christ wanted them to witness that the painful process had purpose, one greater than even alleviating their grief and heartache.

Our Savior not only conquered death for our salvation, but He also returned to bring resurrection power through the Holy Spirit to us collectively, as His body, His bride, the fellowship of believers known as the church. Many church historians and theologians consider Pentecost, when believers gathered for prayer and worship and received the gift of the Holy Spirit, the pivot point for the birth of the church. Without the crushing of the cross, we would not know the resurrection power of Pentecost.

1) Why do you suppose Jesus went out of His way to show Himself to His followers in so many different times and places after His resurrection?

_____

_____

_____

_____

2) Read Acts 2, the story of Pentecost, in your favorite translation of the Bible. What strikes you most about this dynamic event? How does this story resonate in your life today?

_____

_____

_____

_____

3) How would you describe your understanding and perception of the Holy Spirit? Are you as comfortable with the Holy Spirit as you are with God the Father and Jesus, His Son? Why or why not?

_____

_____

_____

_____

_____

Anyone who perseveres and succeeds in fulfilling their life's purpose has almost certainly endured the dark, shameful, excruciating path of crushing. They failed, they suffered, they experienced death—and then, through God's power and their willingness to rise and remove the shroud of their past, they too began to come to life again. They begin to realize that they are different people, stronger and better and more capable of seeing what is true about who they are and why they are on this earth.

You and I are no different. As followers of Jesus, we share in the tearful trail of Calvary, carrying the personalized crosses that threaten to kill us. But then we, too, experience Christ's resurrection power coursing through us. We sense the potent fermenting taking place in the remains of who we once were before our crushing. We begin to realize that there is new life on the other side of the old, pre-crushing life we used to know.

The cross of our shame felt like it would kill us. Every failed relationship, scandal, bankruptcy, conviction, resignation, and bad decision felt like death. But now we know the hope that comes from the eternal life we have in Jesus Christ. Like the apostle Paul, we know that it is this hope that makes us no longer ashamed (Rom. 5:5). Hope promises us that what we thought would kill us only made us stronger.

1) What tangible object in your possession reminds you of how far you have come in your faith? How did it come to be in your life? Why is it still meaningful?

_____

_____

_____

_____

2) What tangible object or material possession continues to haunt you with shame over past failures, mistakes, or transgressions? How can it become a trophy of God's triumphant power in your life?

_____

_____

_____

_____

3) Do you agree that hope is the antidote for shame? Why or why not?

_____

_____

_____

_____

Throughout our lives, we all have our crosses to bear: past abuse, a chronic illness, unrelenting debt, the trauma of unexpected loss. We all go through such times of crushing, but we must never forget our crushing is not the end. From the vineyard where our fruit is crushed into juice we go to the vat of fermentation, the vat of victory. Once we have fermented, then we begin to realize that there is more ahead.

Our new wine must now be contained in new configurations. We are not who we used to be and not yet fully who we will one day become. Just as wine must be funneled from the vats into bottles in order to be stored, shipped, purchased, and enjoyed, we also find ourselves poured into new containers. After our crushing we may find it's time to start a new relationship, a new joy, a new lifestyle, a new ministry.

In order to move forward, however, we must realize that we cannot go back. Things will never be as they once were before our crushing. Jesus said, "No one sews a patch of unshrunk cloth on an old garment, for the patch will pull away from the garment, making the tear worse. Neither do people pour new wine into old wineskins. If they do, the skins will burst; the wine will run out and the wineskins will be ruined. No, they pour new wine into new wineskins, and both are preserved" (Matt. 9:16–17).

Your pain has now been fermented into new wine. You will never change the past. You cannot undo what has been done or reclaim all that has been lost. Instead, you have something new to offer, something with much more power, richer and more delicious in flavor. No longer can you live as crushed fruit because now you are God's new wine, ready to be tasted and served.

1) What remnants or old wineskins do you need to relinquish in order to make room for the new wine you're becoming? What has caused you to resist giving them up prior to now?

_____

_____

_____

_____

2) What does it mean for you to see yourself as God's new wine? In other words, how can you see yourself differently in light of the crushing you've endured?

_____

_____

_____

_____

3) What personal gifts, talents, abilities, and strengths will contribute to the flavor of your new wine? How will you use all that God has given you in order to serve others?

_____

_____

_____

_____

CHAPTER 11

Spiritual Fermentation

Visiting the Holy Land moved me for many reasons, but one of the most powerful moments occurred when I witnessed Jewish people at the Wailing Wall in Jerusalem rocking in place as they prayed. Our guide noticed my curiosity and explained that they rocked that way to honor how God moved with the people of Israel as they traversed through the wilderness on the way to the Promised Land. Even when they wandered, rebelled, and betrayed Him, God lived and moved among them, providing for them and guiding them.

As we begin to see our crushing from God's perspective, I believe we, too, must recognize how God has been with us the entire time. His hand and presence have remained in our lives no matter how lonely, isolated, or afraid we may have felt. God has promised never to leave us or forsake us, and this promise gives us hope in the midst of our crushing but also as we transition into His new wine.

1) What aspects of Judaic culture intrigue you or have caught your attention in the past? How do you relate to these practices from another culture? How do they resonate with your own faith?

_____

_____

_____

2) How has God moved with you throughout your own times of wandering in the wilderness of life? Could you sense Him at the time or just now as you look back?

_____

_____

_____

_____

3) How do you feel when you sense God's presence? Peaceful? Excited? Calm? Energized? Something else?

_____

_____

_____

_____

In order to discover more of who we have become because of our crushing, we not only must rely on God's power through His Holy Spirit but we must also spend more time getting to know Him. God is our Creator, our Heavenly Father, our Redeemer, and the Lover of our souls. Knowing that He wants us to spend time with Him, to know Him and to trust Him like never before, we begin to realize that He satisfies us in ways that nothing else can.

Focused on God as the source of all we need, we prioritize accordingly. Even when we want to be alone with Him, however, it doesn't mean it's easy. Our culture often discourages us from being alone in productive, soul-satisfying, undistracted ways. With online technology and social media, we can stay connected 24/7. We can also stay distracted, interrupted, and frazzled 24/7 as well. Unfortunately, when we're surrounded by people and always diverting our attention to the urgent instead of the eternal, we miss out on what we know we need and want most.

In fact, I'm convinced certain blessings and assets are found only in rest. When I still my soul before God, I think my best thoughts and find more peace in my heart. I also discover that it is during those times that the Father loves to speak, without distractions and disturbances interfering. My experience is not unique, and I believe that during these intervals God often reveals His will. As we learn to rely on Him more and to hear His voice and follow His guidance, our new wine ferments into full maturity and flavor.

1) Are you more of an extrovert and enjoy being with people most of the time? Or are you more of an introvert and need time alone to recharge? Regardless of which one you may tend to be, how does this aspect of your personality affect your relationship with God?

_____

_____

_____

_____

2) How comfortable are you spending time alone with God? How often do you make it a point to spend time with Him?

_____

_____

_____

_____

3) Other than Scripture, what helps you get closer to God? Talking to others about Him? Reading books to inspire your faith? Listening to music or singing worship songs? Something else?

_____

_____

_____

_____

Remember that making wine is a process. Don't overlook the fact that most wine, once bottled, is allowed to rest, to settle, usually in a cool, temperature-controlled environment such as a wine cellar or wine vault. Similarly, we must also allow ourselves to catch our breath after our crushing, fully regaining our strength before venturing in the new direction to which God calls us.

During this time of rest and final fermentation, we also discover the sweetness of true intimacy with God. He doesn't merely free us and transform us just to refine us of our impurities and selfishness. No, He removes those distractions, obstacles, and sediments in our lives so we can be closer to Him, more aware of His presence, more grateful for His blessings, and more attuned to His Spirit. God frees us to worship Him and praise Him, the ultimate purpose for which we are all created.

1) Other than sleep, what are some ways you typically rest? What allows you to relax and recharge?

_____

_____

_____

_____

2) When was the last time you set aside specifically to rest and reflect on your relationship with God? How would you describe that time together?

_____

_____

_____

_____

3) Looking at your schedule for the next week, find at least thirty minutes to block off for you to spend doing nothing but relaxing and enjoying quality time with the Lord.

_____

_____

_____

_____

Our relationship with God, especially at this new level of intimacy, is comparable to a romantic relationship. After all, the church is the bride of Christ. Therefore, it shouldn't surprise us that we can see the pattern of God's wooing, both in the history of His relationship with the people of Israel but also in our individual lives. But even as we begin to grow, recognize new growth in ourselves, and experience a deeper love and dependence on God, we still sometimes struggle.

Like someone jilted at the altar on their wedding day, we might harbor a tinge of fear, skepticism, and doubt that we will yet be crushed. We might be tempted to listen to the enemy of our souls, who wants us to believe God is not good, not for us, and therefore should not be trusted—when, in fact, just the opposite is true. God is always good, always for our good, and always to be trusted.

Just as God pursued Israel and brought her out of bondage and into the Promised Land, He has brought you out of your own place of oppression—your addiction, your abuse, your pain, your loss. But once He opens the Red Sea for your own personal exodus, you must continue to trust Him even if you're still wandering in the wilderness, trying to follow Him to your next destination. You might feel disoriented at times and long for old, sinful comforts—former lovers, shopping, working too much, prescription medications, or some other vehicles of temporary escape. But these are not to be trusted, and eventually you must confront your growing pains and forge a new path by following God.

1) What ongoing fears and anxieties prevent you from deepening your intimacy with God? How can you surrender these to Him and know that He has your future in the palm of His hand?

_____

_____

_____

_____

2) When have you sensed God wooing and pursuing you? How does it make you feel to know He loves you like no other?

_____

_____

_____

_____

3) What currently stands in the way of you going deeper in your commitment to loving and serving God? What will it cost you to move this obstacle or eliminate this barrier?

_____

_____

_____

_____

_____

The movement of God in step with His people did not end when they reached the Promised Land. In fact, it was just beginning. While He moved with the children of Israel in the wilderness during their wandering, in the New Testament, we see God walking among His people through the Incarnation as God took human form in Jesus Christ. Finally, through the gift of the Holy Spirit at Pentecost, we see how God resides in His people, moving through them to advance His kingdom.

God still moves with us and in us and through us today. His presence has always permeated our paths. Now as we begin to shift our perspective on crushing, we experience the indwelling of His Spirit and recognize the transformation taking place within us. None of our suffering is wasted. We are fermenting in order to be something we could never be on our own. Instead of earthly fruit we have become heavenly wine.

1) In what ways has your view of crushing, suffering, and pain changed since you began reading *Crushing* and completing this study guide? What has made the biggest impact on you so far? Why?

_____

_____

_____

_____

2) How willing are you to trust God with your future? With where you will be a year from now? A week from now? An hour from now? Is it easier for you to trust Him with your long-term future or short-term, immediate future? Why?

_____

_____

_____

_____

CHAPTER 12

An Eternal Pairing

Enjoying the taste of a fine wine is unlike any other experience. Typically, the finer the wine, the more subtle and complex the various notes of flavor will delight the palate. Great wine is typically not meant to be enjoyed by itself but instead to be paired with the perfect menu in order to consummate the culinary marriage of food and drink. The wine complements and enhances the spices, herbs, and flavors in the food beyond what they could be if served alone or with a different beverage.

Certain fine wines typically pair better with some meals more than others. Traditionally, red wines pair best with bolder, savory red-meat dishes while white wines complement fish, seafood, and chicken. You want a wine that complements and even enhances the food while possessing its own intensity and flavor. Much in the same way, when we ferment into eternal wine, our pairing with God releases the fullness of our new, bold flavor.

1) When have you particularly enjoyed the taste of wine? How would you describe it? If you have never tasted wine, what do you imagine it tastes like? What is this impression based upon?

_____

_____

_____

_____

2) If you enjoy wine with your meals, what is your favorite combination? What kind of wine do you enjoy accompanying your favorite dinner?

_____

_____

_____

_____

3) What other kinds of pairings come to mind when you think about the perfect way wine and food usually go together? For instance, salt and pepper. What pairing best describes the way you feel you and God relate? Why?

_____

_____

_____

_____

Our pairing with God reflects the eternal nature of our lives. He made us as eternal, spiritual beings housed within temporal, mortal bodies. From the moment of our conception in the womb, we were made to live with God forever.

Because our time on earth is temporary, however, we often lose sight of this truth. Instead, we become consumed and blinded by the visible, tangible elements around us, losing sight of the invisible, eternal realities within the ultimate scope of God's kingdom. Due to our human limitations and the short time we walk this earth, we may doubt our eternal nature and God's intention for us.

Instead, we may allow our limited understanding of temporary pain to drive us into the arms of pleasurable idols that will never be able to appreciate the eternal vintage that makes us so unique. Like the people of Israel creating a golden calf to worship, we chase after drugs, sex, money, fame, and anything else we can find to distract us from the Master Vintner's pursuit as we resist the discomfort required by our crushing.

1) What struggles, temptations, or addictions have chronically hindered your attempts to grow in your faith? How have they pulled you away from God? And how have they driven you toward Him?

_____

_____

_____

_____

2) What object or material item best symbolizes your own personal golden calf or idol? A new designer purse? A house in a certain neighborhood? A corner office? A luxury automobile? Something else?

_____

_____

_____

_____

3) How do you feel when you consider that God made you to be an eternal, spiritual being? How does this shape your view of your relationship with Him right now?

_____

_____

_____

_____

Sometimes our transformation into eternal wine seems delayed. We impatiently struggle to follow the wilderness path of detours and derailments that send us through the desert instead of along a straight course to our divine destination. When the path doesn't seem to reveal itself the way we wish, we might be tempted to believe, yet again, that God has orphaned us in this new, unfamiliar territory.

I suspect, though, that just because we can't see God, it doesn't mean that He's absent. Rather, He may simply be revealing Himself to us in a form we have yet to recognize. We recall how even Christ's disciples first thought Jesus must be a ghost when they saw Him walking on water toward their storm-tossed boat. They weren't used to seeing their Master doing something they deemed impossible, so therefore they couldn't recognize Him.

We often wrestle with the same misperceptions and mistaken assumptions. In the moments of fear and waves of grief from past losses, we lose sight of God's presence in the form we want or are used to seeing. We jump to the conclusion that He is hiding from us or leaving us behind when, in fact, He is simply wanting us to recognize Him in new forms—much like seeing how what was once a grape can be present in wine.

1) What internal process would you like to speed up in order to hasten your maturity? Why?

_____

_____

_____

_____

2) When have you felt like you could not see God's presence in your life or like He was hiding from you?

_____

_____

_____

_____

3) When has God revealed Himself in a new, unfamiliar form that surprised you? How did this revelation change the way you perceive Him? Your relationship with Him?

_____

_____

_____

_____

The delay, at least from our human perspective, in the fulfillment of God's promises is often the source of our pain. I'm convinced that most of the time when the Lord reveals where He wants to take us, He spotlights the mountaintops and leaves the valleys hidden in shadows. He knows that if we could see what we must endure in order to reach those summits, we might give up altogether.

God doesn't want to torture us, tease us, or Taser us with unseen crushing ahead. Instead, He uses those valleys to equip us, strengthen us, and empower us for the steep climbs ahead. In those darkest, most desolate times when we hit rock bottom, we must take comfort that there is something we are gaining that God deems necessary for what lies ahead. We need not abandon our journey but simply forge onward through the storm and trust that blue skies await just beyond the next bend.

1) Have you ever experienced delays and distractions only to realize that God was using them to guide you toward Him?

_____

_____

_____

_____

2) Have you ever waited and desired something for so long that you resolved in yourself that it was never going to happen? Have you ever had to declare that your dreams were dead so that you would finally have a moment's peace?

_____

_____

_____

_____

3) What sustains your faith in God right now? Why do you continue to trust Him after all you've endured and suffered in your life?

_____

_____

_____

_____

Many times, your crushing leaves you raw and vulnerable so that even as God begins to rebuild your dreams, you're tempted to run. Keep in mind, however, the central message of what we've been discussing throughout Crushing as well as this study guide. The crushing you experience in life's dark valleys become the resurrection tools God uses to bring you new life atop the peaks of success.

Just as Christ endured the pain before His gain, we too must give ourselves over to this process—especially as we come out the other side of our crushing into fermentation. As we adjust to being new wine, we must resist retreating back to the familiar, default ways of hopelessness, resignation, and despair. Every delay, setback, discouragement, or reminder of past losses can be used as God's building blocks to breathe new life into your dreams.

As you grow accustomed to being new wine, you must realize that you will see God in new ways as well. Your pairing with Him goes beyond the perfection of a fine wine sipped during the consumption of a gourmet meal. Your pairing with God is literally an eternal match made in heaven.

1) When circumstances in your life get hard, are you more inclined toward fight or flight? Do you like to confront problems head-on? Or run from them in hopes they will disappear?

_____

_____

_____

_____

2) What do you fear losing most in your life right now? How does this fear inhibit your faith from maturing? How do you live with this fear in the midst of trusting God with your future?

_____

_____

_____

_____

CHAPTER 13

A Tasting with the King

Wine tastings have become a popular way to enjoy a unique social experience. Participants can enjoy sharing the same beverage and comparing notes on their response to its taste. They can exchange knowledge of various wines and how the one at hand fairs by comparison.

These gatherings are pleasant and enjoyable, I'm sure. But I suspect they simply cannot compare with the rather wild, rambunctious parties, feasts, and festivals held during harvest season in ancient Israel. Celebratory in nature, these events not only commemorated Jewish history but also reminded people of all God had done for them.

1) Have you ever attended a wine tasting? How would you describe it? Would you go again? If you've never been to one, would you want to? Why or why not?

_____

_____

_____

_____

2) What is your gold standard for a good party or holiday celebration? What ingredients and people must be included in order for you to enjoy yourself as much as possible?

_____

_____

_____

_____

3) When was the last time you celebrated a milestone, attended an event, or participated in hosting a party? What did you enjoy most about this time? What disappointed you the most about it?

_____

_____

_____

_____

During its antiquity as a civilization, Israel was largely an agrarian society. Celebrating God's tangible blessings in the form of their harvests, the Hebrew people kept seven feasts: the Feast of Passover, the Feast of Unleavened Bread, the Feast of Firstfruits, the Feast of Weeks (Pentecost), the Feast of Trumpets (Rosh Hashanah), the Day of Atonement (Yom Kippur), and the Feast of Tabernacles. While each of these commemorated a major milestone of God's presence and provision for Israel, I suspect these feasts also celebrated what God would continue to do for His people.

Even as Israel celebrated all God had done on their behalf, I wonder if perhaps God enjoyed celebrating His people at the same time. I suspect He did and still does as we individually ferment into faithfulness that's stronger, bolder, and more potent than the juice we once were. After fermentation, God surely celebrates the fulfillment of our potential by inviting others to sip and enjoy what He has produced in our lives. These celebrations must surely include the rowdiest, loudest, and most worshipful occasions we can imagine.

1) Do you agree that God celebrates us as much as we celebrate what He has done in our lives? Why or why not?

_____

_____

_____

_____

2) When have you sensed God's pleasure in your life, a sense that He is pleased with your growth, progress, and maturity? What led to your awareness of Him celebrating how far you have come?

_____

_____

_____

_____

3) How does remembering all that God has done for you at regular intervals or seasons of the year strengthen your faith? How do such occasions help you overcome fears about your future? Why?

_____

_____

_____

_____

Our Master Vintner patterns our perfection into wine after the process we see in the life, death, and resurrection of His Son, Jesus. Just as Christ ascended into heaven to be with His Father after revealing Himself after the resurrection, we now move into a new level of intimate connection with our Heavenly Father. We have no need to rely on blood sacrifices and temple priests now that we have the sacrifice Christ made on the cross that gives us direct access to God. We can now move into the presence of God personally and directly.

We can move beyond the temple's outer court and walk directly into God's presence in the Holy of Holies. There, as His new and eternal wine, we offer ourselves to be poured for His pleasure. We enjoy the consummating consumption of being new wine fit for the King of Kings, knowing He wants to share His creation, us, with others in His kingdom.

Here, in the presence of the Living God, we exist as His wine for all eternity. We now enjoy the intimacy and communion the Lover of our souls has sought to fulfill with us since Adam and Eve first sinned in the Garden of Eden. Before our Lord and Savior, we finally grasp who we truly are and bask in the fullness of His love. We see the process completed as our Master Vintner has moved us from an outer court crushing, an inner court refinement, and into His presence in the Holiest of Holies for all eternity.

1) If you were to map the highs and lows of your walk with God throughout your life, what would it look like? Use the space below to sketch or doodle a map, graph, picture, or some other illustration of this ongoing process.

2) What difference does it make in your life on a daily basis that you have direct access to intimacy with God?

_____

_____

_____

_____

3) When have you felt closest to God and knew you were enjoying a sacred time with Him?

_____

_____

_____

_____

When we embrace being God's new creation in Christ and get used to being His new wine, we experience new levels of peace, joy, contentment, and satisfaction. We know our true purpose and delight in living it out, sharing our gifts, and serving others because of all that God has done for us.

From time to time, tiny sediments of the past may attempt to derail your progress, but you only have to run to God to remember what is true. You are no longer who you once were but are becoming all your Creator ever wanted you to be. You are now God's trophy instead of the victim of circumstance you once believed.

Like any proud parent or happy vintner, God delights in you and the new wine you have become. Elated with your unique and special vintage, He keeps you close in His personal winery while also sharing you with the world as an example of the miracle He has done in your life. Sour grapes were crushed into sweet juice in order that delicious wine could be made.

The Master Vintner wants others to savor the flavor He has produced in you, His new creation. You now have His power within you. You now have full access to all the riches in Christ and the power of His Holy Spirit. Consequently, God wants you to offer hope to those being crushed and struggling to understand what is happening to them. He wants you to comfort the lonely, heal the sick, strengthen the weak, and reveal the light of His love in a dark world. You are God's most exquisite vintage of eternal wine.

1) After experiencing a spiritual growth spurt or mountaintop experience with God, when have you immediately encountered an obstacle, barrier, or setback? Does knowing these temporary delays often follow times of growth change your perspective on them?

_____

_____

_____

_____

2) What is God's greatest accomplishment in your life? If you were to share your testimony right now, what would you say? What's the most dramatic change in you thanks to walking with the Lord?

_____

_____

_____

_____

3) When have you been used by God as a conduit for His power? What was the outcome? How did He use your unique abilities, gifts, and talents to reflect His glory?

_____

_____

_____

_____

CHAPTER 14

The Wedding Planner

Weddings are unique occasions of celebration. Uniting two families, these community events fulfill the promise of new love, new life, and new hope for the future. From ancient times to our modern, twenty-first-century ceremonies, weddings provide the perfect opportunity for celebrating the power of God's love to triumph over adversity. No wonder then that in the Bible we find Jesus' first miracle to be a simple act that transforms a wedding party into a one-of-a-kind celebration.

1) When was the last time you attended a wedding? What was your experience like? How would you describe it?

_____

_____

_____

_____

2) What do you enjoy most about attending a wedding? Least?

_____

_____

_____

_____

If you or I were the Messiah, I suspect most of us would not have chosen to be the beverage supplier at a wedding as our first miracle. Nonetheless, this is exactly what Jesus ended up doing. He could have chosen any display of His power, any revelation of His identity as God's Son, and yet He chose to protect the dignity of a family hosting a joyful wedding reception. Let's take a look at how it happened:

> On the third day a wedding took place at Cana in Galilee. Jesus' mother was there, and Jesus and his disciples had also been invited to the wedding. When the wine was gone, Jesus' mother said to him, "They have no more wine."
> "Woman, why do you involve me?" Jesus replied. "My hour has not yet come."
> His mother said to the servants, "Do whatever he tells you."
> Nearby stood six stone water jars, the kind used by the Jews for ceremonial washing, each holding from twenty to thirty gallons.
> Jesus said to the servants, "Fill the jars with water"; so they filled them to the brim.
> Then he told them, "Now draw some out and take it to the master of the banquet."
> They did so, and the master of the banquet tasted the water that had been turned into wine. He did not realize where it had come from, though the servants who had drawn the water knew. Then he called the bridegroom aside and said, "Everyone brings out the choice wine first and then the cheaper wine after the guests have had too much to drink; but you have saved the best till now."
> (John 2:1–10)

This scene reminds us that so often God rescues us from what could have happened or even should have happened. Running out of wine at a wedding reception may not strike us as a crisis of epic proportions, but at that time, culturally and socially it was. Prompted by His mother, Mary, Jesus goes into action and produces the most exquisite bouquet of vintage wine ever tasted. And no one there even knew He was responsible.

Frequently, the Master Vintner's power in our lives fills deficits we didn't even know we had. Others may not realize that God is responsible for the changes in us until we tell them directly. They may have noticed how we have softened and grown wiser, stronger, and more resilient. But they may not grasp the catalyst for our transformation into eternal wine until we reveal our Vintner's label.

1) What phrase or detail stands out to you in this passage about Jesus' first miracle? How does it speak into your life right now?

_____

_____

_____

_____

2) What surprises you most about how this miracle occurs? Why?

_____

_____

_____

3) Can you relate to Mary's need to prompt Jesus into action? When was the last time you rushed to tell God what He needed to do?

_____

_____

_____

_____

4) Why do you suppose Christ chose this occasion to perform His first miracle? What significance does it have that it's set at a wedding? Why?

_____

_____

_____

_____

_____

We usually have the tendency to rush the Lord when we discover a problem in our lives. As soon as we have a need, a want, or a crisis, we pray and want immediate results. From our limited understanding and perception, it's almost as if we assume we need to inform God of our problem—as if He doesn't already know.

Perhaps we see a glimpse of this urgency in the reaction of Mary when she realizes the wine has run out. Make no mistake, it's not that Mary ever doubted her Son's ability to provide new wine—it's that in her haste she may have presumed to have a better grasp on the problem than He did. Like all of us, she may have felt inclined to prompt God to solve a problem based on our knowledge and experience of it.

But the Lord doesn't need us to sound an alarm or inform Him of what needs to be done. He who formed the vast void of empty space into the heavens and the earth knows all, sees all, and accomplishes all His purposes—in His perfect timing. Even as we celebrate God's healing presence in our lives, we must be careful not to rush ahead of what He's doing with us and how He wants to use us.

1) When have you tried to run ahead of God and rush the outcome you believed He was producing? What did He teach you from that experience?

_____

_____

_____

_____

2) When have you experienced God's perfect timing in your life? How did His timing differ from how you would have arranged the timing of this event?

_____

_____

_____

3) Knowing all you've seen God do in your life, why is it still difficult for you to wait for His timing? In what ways is it easier for you now than it used to be?

_____

_____

_____

In such moments of depletion and urgent need, we must remember that everything God does is perfectly strategic. We will never witness God running late for any of His divine appointments with His children. Jesus did not need His mother to tell Him to change the water into wine. Perhaps, instead, God was doing something in Mary that required her to stretch her faith as she called her Son to use His almighty power in that moment.

Therefore, we cling to our faith and trust God to work in His vast omniscient wisdom—not in our limited human understanding of a situation. We hold fast in our belief that His timing is perfect—even when we want it sooner or fail to understand why He chooses to act when He does. God wants to develop us through a process of maturation into His wine, and so it seems likely that He then uses our new flavorful potency as only He knows best. While there are times in our lives when He instantly brings forth in us what is necessary at that moment, God also takes the time necessary for maximum eternal impact.

1) Is it easier for you to assure other people that God's timing is perfect or to wait for God's timing in your own life? What accounts for the difference?

_____

_____

_____

_____

2) Do you consider yourself a punctual person who tends to be early to appointments? Or are you usually running late because you're pulled in so many directions? How does your own tendency skew the way you view God's timing?

_____

_____

_____

_____

3) If you could have an immediate response, answer, or provision from God at this very moment, what would you ask from Him? Why?

_____

_____

_____

_____

Without the intervention of the Master Vintner, we would all remain nothing more than water at a wedding where wine is needed. The wedding at Cana reminds us that our worth is not found in what we do and who we are when left to our own devices and desires. Instead, our priceless value derives from what God does with us, His new creation. Therefore, we continually grow in this realization, even after we're fermented, and must resist the human tendency toward immediate gratification and instant solutions.

You may be struggling with such a tendency right now. You have seen God's hand in the process of your crushing and fermentation and know that He is using you to accomplish His purposes. So why would you dare assume that He doesn't know when to serve you up for us to taste and to celebrate? From my experience and what I see in Scripture as well as the lives of others, God always saves His best for last.

If Jesus can use the lack of wine at a wedding feast for His glory while preventing a family's public embarrassment and shame, I believe that He will use the smallest details of your life to propel you forward as He advances His kingdom. His party has already started. The old wine has passed, and now His new wine, you, is being served. Your crushing is never the end because the best is yet to come.

1) When was the last time you celebrated God's goodness in your life with the people you love the most? What did you love most about that occasion?

_____

_____

_____

_____

2) When is the next opportunity you can gather family and friends in order to celebrate together? How can you use your time together to reveal how God is currently moving in your life? Consider one way you can show your loved ones how God has changed you in the past year.

_____

_____

_____

_____

CHAPTER 15

New Wine

Your crushing is never the end. In the midst of your most brutally painful moments, God is still there with you. Not only is He present to comfort, hold, and reassure you, but He is also up to something you cannot yet see. As He rebuilds and restores you, eventually you will glimpse that there's more going on, both within and beyond you, than you could have previously imagined.

You begin to realize amid life's ups and downs that God remains uniquely persistent in His desire to transform us. He never gives up on us and refuses to abandon us even when we attempt to run away from Him. Like the loving Father He is, God simply allows us to run until we reach the end of ourselves. Then, as we come to our senses like the prodigal does in the parable Jesus tells (Luke 15:11–32), we realize just how much our waiting Heavenly Father loves us. He runs to meet us every time.

1) Read the parable of the prodigal son in Luke 15:11–32 in your favorite translation of the Bible. With whom do you identify the most: the father, the prodigal, or the elder brother? Why?

_____

_____

_____

_____

2) With this passage in mind, what has God used in your past times of crushing to help you come to your senses and return home to Him?

_____

_____

_____

_____

3) How has God revealed His loving care for you in the midst of your most recent crushing crisis?

_____

_____

_____

_____

God's plan has always been more elaborately intricate than we previously realized. His goal includes but is not limited to saving us from the punishment due from our sinful rebellion. He loves us, and His unconditional love compels Him to be the focus of His beloved. With love as His motivation, He nonetheless grants us free will so that we get to choose how we will respond to His wooing, relentless pursuit.

As we experience the consequences of going our own way, God loves us so much that He then uses this crushing to get our attention and return our gaze to Him. By allowing pain to enter our lives, God is not out to destroy us but to save us from ourselves. He wants to remake us, remold us, and reshape us into something that looks just like Him.

In order to accomplish such an audacious transformation, God, our Master Vintner, becomes part of the vineyard of our humanity. In the form of a man named Jesus, God planted Himself as the True Vine from which we, His branches, would grow. Through this grafting process, we no longer wither and die but instead produce fruit fit for crushing into fermented, everlasting wine.

1) In what ways have you changed the most in your adult life? What has produced these changes? How have you seen God work in the midst of them?

_____

_____

_____

_____

2) Based on what you've read in *Crushing* and what God has revealed to you through this study, how will you view your new crisis, calamity, or catastrophe differently from you would have beforehand?

_____

_____

_____

_____

3) What change would you like to see God make in your life next? Why?

_____

_____

_____

_____

No matter where you are in the process of your crushing, fermenting, and serving, you can trust that God is always at work. If you're suffering the devastation of an unbearable burden, then take comfort in knowing that your pain has a higher purpose. If you're biding time and waiting on God to act or to reveal Himself in a way you can recognize, then remain vigilant. Trust that His timing is divinely perfect and will synchronize events in ways that you will never fully comprehend while you're on this earth.

Regardless of where you are in the process or whether you believe all that I've shared about crushing, I pray you will never give up. You must hold on and wait for the Lord. Dare to believe that He would not have brought you this far only to abandon you now.

Dare to hope that He is allowing you to go through all that you've experienced in order to be the precious, priceless vintage He wants to produce.

1) What stage of the crushing process has resonated the most with where you see yourself right now? Which chapter of _Crushing_ has meant the most to you or been used by God to speak to your heart?

_____

_____

_____

_____

2) How has this journey through _Crushing_ and this study changed the way you see your past? Your present? Your future?

_____

_____

_____

_____

_____

3) How would you summarize what you have gained from completing this study? What difference has it made in your daily life?

_____

_____

_____

_____

As we conclude this journey together, I commend you for exploring the depths of your soul in order to become all that God made you to be. Whether you see it at this moment or not, you are now proof pointing others to the God who loves and wants to transform each of us. You are His eternal wine, worth all the pain, turmoil, and suffering required to produce the metamorphosis into His masterpiece. Your pain is but a temporary affliction compared with the exquisite glory of what God is doing in your life.

You have something to offer the world that no one else has. You are fearfully and wonderfully made in the image of God. He wants you to fulfill the divine potential He has planted within your DNA. He will do whatever it takes for you to reach this level of exceptional, eternal maturity. You are a work in progress toward the powerful, passionate, purposeful person He intended you to be before you were ever born.

Don't give up now! Not when you are so close to becoming wine.

Crushing is not the end—it's your new beginning!

1) On a scale of 1 to 10, with 1 being completely skeptical and 10 being 100 percent certain, how convinced are you that crushing is not the end? How has your view of crushing changed in the past few weeks? Why?

_____

_____

_____

_____

2) What's the biggest takeaway you will carry with you from this exploration of your life's most painful moments?

_____

_____

_____

_____

3) What one action can you take today to demonstrate your deeper faith in God's goodness in your life? How can you take what you've learned and use it to serve others every day?

_____

_____

_____

_____

About the Author

T. D. Jakes is a number one *New York Times* bestselling author of more than forty books and is the CEO of TDJ Enterprises, LLP. He is the founder of the thirty-thousand-member Potter's House Church, and his television ministry program, *The Potter's Touch,* is watched by 3.3 million viewers every week. He has produced Grammy Award–winning music and such films as *Heaven Is for Real, Sparkle,* and *Jumping the Broom.* A master communicator, he hosts MegaFest, Woman Thou Art Loosed, and other conferences attended by tens of thousands. T. D. Jakes lives in Dallas with his wife and five children. Visit www.tdjakes.com.